by Tracy White

photography

FOR SCRAPBOOKERS

A LEISURE ARTS PUBLICATION

EDITOR-IN-CHIEF Tracy White
SPECIAL PROJECTS EDITOR Leslie Miller
MANAGING EDITOR Marianne Madsen
EDITOR-AT-LARGE Jana Lillie
SENIOR WRITERS Brittany Beattie, Denise Pauley, Rachel Thomae
SENIOR EDITOR, SPECIAL PROJECTS Vanessa Hoy
ASSOCIATE EDITOR Jennifer Purdie
ASSOCIATE WRITER Lori Fairbanks
ASSISTANT EDITOR Britney Mellen
COPY EDITOR Kim Sandoval
EDITORIAL ASSISTANTS Joannie McBride, Fred Brewer, Liesl Russell
PHOTOGRAPHY CONSULTANT Candice Stringham
ART DIRECTOR Brian Tippetts
ASSOCIATE ART DIRECTOR, SPECIAL PROJECTS Erin Bayless
PUBLISHER Tony Golden
FOUNDING EDITOR Lisa Bearnson
VICE PRESIDENT, GROUP PUBLISHER David O'Neil
SVP, GROUP PUBLISHING DIRECTOR Scott Wagner

PRIMEDIA
Consumer Magazine & Internet Group

CHAIRMAN, CEO & PRESIDENT Dean Nelson
VICE CHAIRMAN Beverly C. Chell

LEISURE ARTS, Inc.
VICE PRESIDENT AND EDITOR-IN-CHIEF Sandra Graham Case
EXECUTIVE DIRECTOR OF PUBLICATIONS Cheryl Nodine Gunnells
SENIOR PUBLICATIONS DIRECTOR Susan White Sullivan
SPECIAL PROJECTS DIRECTOR Susan Frantz Wiles
DIRECTOR OF RETAIL MARKETING Stephen Wilson
DIRECTOR OF DESIGNER RELATIONS Debra Nettles
SENIOR ART OPERATIONS DIRECTOR Jeff Curtis
ART IMAGING DIRECTOR Mark Hawkins
PUBLISHING SYSTEMS ADMINISTRATOR Becky Riddle
PUBLISHING SYSTEMS ASSISTANTS Clint Hanson and John Rose
PUBLISHING SYSTEMS INTERNS Shannon Connell and Josh Hyatt

CHIEF OPERATING OFFICER Tom Siebenmorgen
DIRECTOR OF CORPORATE PLANNING AND DEVELOPMENT Laticia Mull Dittrich
VICE PRESIDENT, SALES AND MARKETING Pam Stebbins
DIRECTOR OF SALES AND SERVICES Margaret Reinold
VICE PRESIDENT, OPERATIONS Jim Dittrich
COMPTROLLER, OPERATIONS Rob Thieme
RETAIL CUSTOMER SERVICE MANAGER Stan Raynor
PRINT PRODUCTION MANAGER Fred F. Pruss

Library of Congress Control Number: 2006920763
White, Tracy
Creating Keepsakes' *Photography for Scrapbookers*
"A Leisure Arts Publication"

ISBN 1-57486-605-2

[CONTENTS]

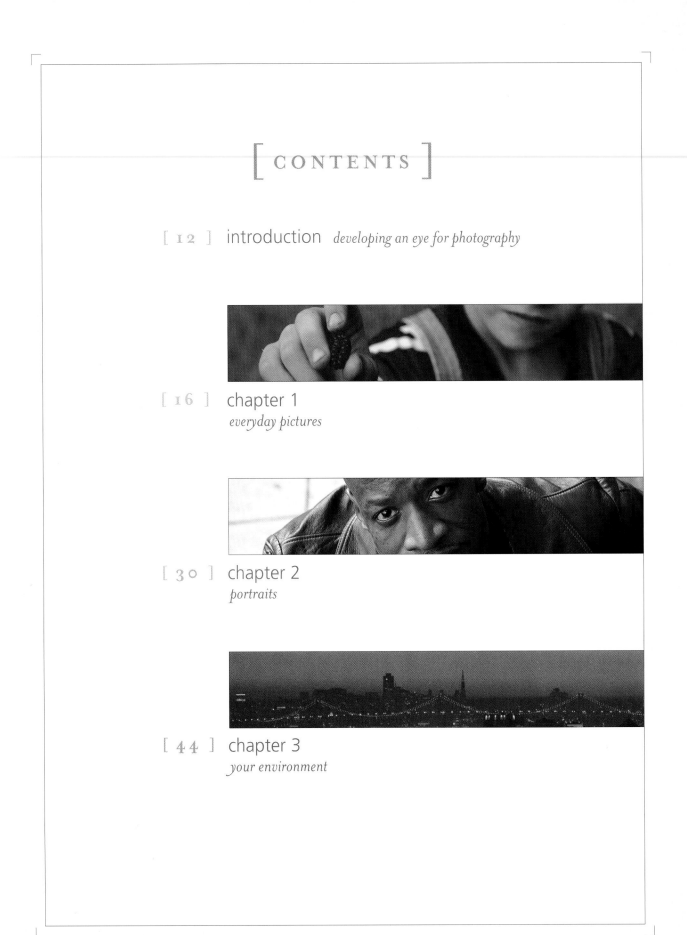

[WANT TO TAKE BETTER PHOTOS? TRY THESE 5 TIPS]

I'll admit it—I'm an avid photographer. Get me behind a camera and I lose track of time. I can whip through several rolls of film (yes, I still use an "old-fashioned" film camera!) in no time; it's as if I'm in my element when I've got a camera strapped around my neck.

When I first started taking photos, my eyes glazed over whenever anyone talked about f-stops and shutter speeds. It all seemed confusing and, really, I just wanted to learn how to take beautiful photos of the people I love and the places I visit.

Well, that's what this book is about. On every page, you'll learn easy tips to help you take "scrapbook-worthy" photos—you know, photos that tell stories and capture the essence of your loved ones. After all, as scrapbookers, we are our families' storytellers—it's our job to capture and preserve the memories we hold dear, and taking better photos is just one way we can do that.

So, you want to take better photos? Here are my top tips—and this book is filled with more of them!

TIP 1

Want to improve your photos? Try this easy (yet oh-so-effective) tip:

1. Pick up your camera and hold it to your eye. (Are you doing it?)

2. Look around the perimeter of the viewfinder. What do you see? Do you see toys on the ground? Do you see that you're cropping out your husband's head as you focus on your little one? Do you see that leaf peeking out from behind your subject's head?

3. Now move the camera around (or recompose) so you eliminate those distractions (making sure you watch for new distractions), then take the shot.

TIP 2

Stand up (yep, I'm serious), then take three giant steps forward. Pretty easy, isn't it? I guarantee you'll get better photos by simply moving closer to your subject.

TIP 3

See those things called knees? Well, not only do they help you walk forward, but they also help you kneel or climb up high. Taking photos from different perspectives will help you take extraordinary images.

TIP 4

Turn off your flash. It sounds contradictory, but in most situations you don't need a flash. Instead, place your subject next to a window or open door and use the natural light to illuminate your subject.

TIP 5

Read your camera's manual. You knew it was coming, but I promise, by understanding your camera, you're going to take better photos. For example, you'll know your camera's limitations (like maybe you can't get super-close photos because of something called a fixed focal length), or maybe you'll learn that you can get better images of your daughter by using the portrait mode on your camera.

But don't just read it today. Reread it in six months, then a year from now. Oh, I'll be the first to admit that it's a "boring" read, but the more you understand photography, the more sense the manual makes.

SO, WHAT'S NEXT?

Will you do me a favor? Here's what I'm asking: practice the tips in this book (get 'em down to the point that they're second nature), then learn about f-stops, shutter speed, depth of field, etc., etc., etc. (Did your eyes glaze over?)

Just as the tips in this book will help you take better photos, being competent with the technical aspects of photography will help you take more creative photos—really.

Now get going. Start telling stories with your camera and be your family's storyteller!

Tracy White

[HOW TO USE THIS BOOK]

If you get only one thing out of this book, I want it to be this:
You can take beautiful photos of your family and friends—and you can do
it today. You don't need a fancy camera, you don't need a semester-long
photography class, and you don't need a professional photo studio.

Your photos are the stars of your layouts! And you want those photos to be their best.
Photography for Scrapbookers is divided into chapters that reflect the kinds of photos
most scrapbookers take:

EVERYDAY PICTURES

You know, the shots you grab the camera for just because your kids are so cute you
have to capture them on film

PORTRAITS

Your subjects looking their best

YOUR ENVIRONMENT

From the small details that make up your home to the magnificent architecture on your
field trip to Washington, D.C.

NATURE AND LANDSCAPE

Close-ups of the flowers in your garden or distant shots of a magnificent sunset over
the lake

HOLIDAYS AND SPECIAL OCCASIONS

Weddings, birthdays, holidays and more

ACTION

Anything from little league to playing in the park

Within each of these chapters, you'll find lots of easy-to-use tips for improving your
photos immediately. Look for photos you particularly like and discover helpful hints about
re-creating the look in your own photographs. I've provided hints on lighting, composition
and more. You'll also find an icon showing which preset mode to use to best capture each
picture. To find out more about each setting, check out the legend at right.

In the back of the book, you'll find an appendix with tips for successfully photographing
specific subjects, such as babies, toddlers, children, teens and adults. You'll also find a
glossary that gives you a basic overview of the technical aspects of photography.

The best way to become a better photographer is simple: take more photographs. As you
continue to study photos and take your own, you can't help but become a better photographer—and you'll have captured many precious memories in the process!

$\big[$ COMMON PRESET CAMERA SETTINGS $\big]$

Wondering which camera setting to use for your photos? Check out how some of the most widely available scene modes work.

 [AUTOMATIC] Aperture and shutter speed are set automatically for a wide variety of shots. This mode is the most reliable setting, though its results can be dull compared to those taken in other modes. Press the shutter button halfway to focus on a subject, then depress it the rest of the way to take the shot.

 [SCENE/LANDSCAPE] Designed to photograph full-frame images at a distant range while keeping the entire scene in focus.

 [PORTRAIT] Captures the foreground subject in clear focus while blurring the background. This mode is most often used for taking pictures of people, though it works well for many types of shots.

 [ACTION] Utilizes a fast shutter speed to freeze the action of fast-moving subjects.

 [CLOSE-UP/MACRO] Used for capturing full-frame images at a very close range. This mode magnifies the details of the objects, though your camera needs to be within a specified distance from the subject (check your camera's manual to find the range).

 [NIGHT] Enables the flash to highlight people in the foreground (if applicable) and uses a long shutter speed to allow more light into the camera to capture the best image in the dark. *Note:* If you're photographing a distant scene without people in the foreground, turn off your flash when using the night setting. This mode works best when used with a tripod.

[SNOW & BEACH] Compensates exposure time for areas prone to reflect a lot of light, such as scenes near snow and beaches, to prevent overexposed photos.

[INTRODUCTION: DEVELOPING AN EYE FOR PHOTOGRAPHY]

Photographs by Tracy White

While writing this book, I brought a stack of photos into the office. A team member thumbed through them and asked, "Tracy, how do your photos turn out so great?" My answer? I've simply trained my eye. I also confessed that I had a separate stack of "ordinary" photos at home—after all, I think we're all allowed to have those photos, too! But I have a lot fewer of those leave-at-home photos than I used to have.

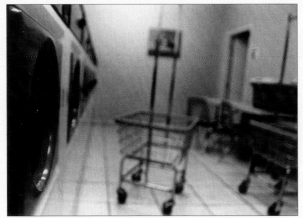
Laundromat objects

Through experience, I've learned when to zoom, when to crouch down or step up, when to turn off my flash, etc. I've learned to not just take pictures, but to see the world in pictures. Literally. As I walk down the street, I notice highlights the sun leaves on stairwells, reflections in windows and glass-paned doors, and—if you can believe it—even beauty in seemingly dull objects in a Laundromat (see my pictures). I notice colors that work well together, patterns and lines that draw the eye, and shadows that produce interesting effects. An obsession? Perhaps, but it's one that simply developed the more I took an interest in taking good photos—photos I am proud to put on my scrapbook pages. I'm not the only one, either. Several friends have said the same thing happened to them when they practiced taking better pictures. They noticed "photo ops" everywhere they went. It will happen to you, too, when you start applying the principles and tips in this book.

A city stairwell   Reflections in a glass-paned door

PAY ATTENTION TO WHAT YOU LIKE

In order to develop an "eye for photography," you have to know your photography style. Without knowing which pictures you like, you'll never be able to *take* pictures you like. So how did I develop my style? And how can you develop yours? Take some time to experiment with these ideas:

- Study ads, billboards and posters that appeal to you. How are the photos on them lit? Composed? Are the subjects close up or far away? Centered or askew? What feelings are captured with the photos?

- Study the work of your favorite photographers. Why are you drawn to their work? Is it the subject matter? Their color sense? The way they capture motion or emotion? Are their photographs beautiful? Artistic? Edgy?

- Experiment constantly. Capture an image three to five different ways—from different vantage points, angles or with varied camera settings to determine which results please you. Five photos may sound like a lot at first, but it's a surefire way to recognize the different results you can create with different approaches. Humor me and try it today (like I did with these cookie photos)—you'll see what I mean.

- Look at your "mistakes." Do you find yourself making the same corrections when post-processing your digital photos or always asking your developer to tweak the same aspect of your prints? Consider altering your shooting style to fix these "errors" before they happen.

- Ask someone else to evaluate your shots. They might uncover common themes and styles.

- Play whenever you get the chance. Shoot a lot of images until you begin to see themes and elements appearing in your favorite pictures. Soon you'll discover ideas, images and techniques that can become your trademark.

The more I look at other people's shots, the more I'm aware of and willing to try different approaches to improve my style. The more I practice, the better I get. As you follow the tips associated with the photos in this book, then practice them, the more you'll love your photos, too.

We'll keep improving together.

When I teach photography classes, people often ask, "How can I create a photo that looks interesting?" The key is photographing something that *is* interesting. Profound, isn't it? Especially when you consider that everything in this world is interesting when viewed with the right perspective. I'm serious. Think of book authors. If they want people to remember their stories, they have to make the stories meaningful. By choosing the right words and placing them in the right setting, these authors create an unforgettable tale from seemingly ordinary events. Photography is the same way. See the photos below? Chairs and common fruits may not have been your first thought for beautiful photo subjects. But by finding the right way to capture them (such as setting the fruit on a light box), I created memorable photographs simply by viewing these everyday items in a new way. I found a story to tell, and I used my camera to tell it.

A chair moved near a window

Each time you get ready to take a picture, decide which story you want to tell. Make it a habit to ask yourself these three basic questions whenever you pull out your camera:

- What do I want the viewer to take from the photograph?
- What is the focus, and how do I create it?
- What feeling do I want to achieve, and how can I reach it by the way I set up my photo?

Only when you know what photo you want to take will your "eye" know what to capture.

After asking yourself these questions, you'll be better prepared to capture an intriguing story. This process of deciding what you want to say and how you want to say it is referred to as "composition." Composition is all about leading the eye where you want it to go. It's as much about what you leave out of the frame as what you leave in. When you look through your camera's viewfinder, pick out details you want to remember and let go of unwanted information that might take away from the focus. Fill the frame with importance.

As you photograph a subject, keep in mind the story you want to tell. This will help you make composition choices that will improve your end result.

Raspberries on a light box

Sliced oranges on a light box

REFINE YOUR EYE

Take five seconds to look away from this book and notice the objects in the room. Now, tell me what you saw. A couch, two chairs, a table, the television. Good. But what else? Did you mention the socks your son left in the corner or the papers sitting on your fireplace mantle? Why not? Because your eye tuned them out. The human eye is amazing! It sees what it wants to see and passes over items it doesn't want to see. A camera, on the other hand, does not have that capability. If you were to take a picture of the room, the photo would reveal the couch, chairs, table and television that you saw, but it would also show every single item you didn't pay attention to.

As you develop your eye for photography, you need to see the way the camera sees. If not, you may end up with photos that aren't quite what you'd pictured when you took them. Case in point: In the pictures below, I've noted a couple of simple changes that would make the photos a little better.

The "horns" become a little distracting, don't you think?
Photograph by Allison Orthner

This picture captures great humor! But did you notice the slanted horizon line (it would look better straight) and the cut-off feet?
Photograph by Joannie McBride

See what I mean? Pay attention to the small details in your photographs before you take them, and make sure you include only the details that are important to the story you want to tell. It's working with the little things that will produce great photos.

PRACTICE, PRACTICE, PRACTICE

So what is your style? I can't answer that for you. But I can tell you how to find it. You'll discover the answers in the tips in this book—tips that will help train your eye. First, look at each photo—the image you should study—and see how it relates to each principle. Then look at the tips; they'll show you how that specific image was composed and teach you how to achieve the same effect when you take the shot. Pull out your own photos and see how they compare. Then grab your camera and start practicing! To paraphrase Wayne Gretzky, you'll miss one-hundred percent of the stunning photos you never take.

chapter 1 everyday pictures

IT'S OFTEN THE LITTLE THINGS THAT MAKE LIFE SO SPECIAL. Going to lunch with close friends. Eating out for dinner instead of cooking at home (or vice versa if you have a busy life!). Going on a walk with family. Grabbing a warm blanket and reading a good book. These are the little things that mean so much.

My life wouldn't be complete without the day-to-day happenings, and neither would my scrapbooks without pictures of these events! But I've learned that everyday shots don't have to look "everyday" and ordinary. By keeping a few simple tips in mind, I can take shots that are as meaningful as the events themselves—and so can you! Just check out my favorite "everyday" tips in this chapter.

[CHOOSE YOUR FOCUS]

Whenever I talk with friends I haven't seen in a while, I want to discuss so many things that I don't have a lot of time to spend telling each story. Instead, I highlight the points that mean the most to me and that tell the events most directly. Sometimes I spend more time on the setting; other times I talk about people I met. Choosing the most important points and focusing on them actually lets me share more details by saying less.

The same is true of photos. Deciding what story or feeling you want to capture, then composing each shot with that specific focus will help you take meaningful photographs.

Focus on cards
Photograph by Sande Krieger

 *Sande's Approach:*

- Crop out any unnecessary background from your photo—it will help viewers determine the focus of the story more quickly.
- To focus on the cards, select the portrait mode on your camera (it will blur the subject in the background while focusing on the subject in the foreground). Focus your viewfinder on the cards and take the picture.

 Sande's Approach:

- If you're photographing indoors, open the windows and use natural light where possible for the best photos.
- To focus on the boy in the shot, use the portrait mode and focus your viewfinder on him, then recompose the shot so the cards are centered and take the picture. If you can control your camera manually, experiment with the aperture to select your desired depth of field. (For more information on aperture and depth of field, see the glossary on page 102.) The manual mode will give you more options with depth of field than most point-and-shoot cameras will.

Focus on boy's face
Photograph by Sande Krieger

the picker

the pumpkin

pickin' a pumpkin

lincoln gardens • October 22, '05 • 4$

PICKIN' A PUMPKIN **by Melissa Chapman**
> **Supplies** *Textured cardstock:* Bazzill Basics Paper and Prism; *Letter die cut:* KI Memories; *Brads:* Bazzill Basics Paper;
Computer font: American Typewriter, downloaded from the Internet.

Melissa's Approach:

- Is the subject you want to focus on close to the ground? Bend down and get on its level! It will create more visual interest and help you capture it in greater focus while letting the other items appear blurred.

- Focusing on objects in the foreground of your picture and placing secondary subjects in the background helps create a nice depth of field.

SIMILAR SITUATIONS

In the following situations, how does the story change when you focus on:

- A child's face or the stuffed animal she's hugging?

- An open book or the person reading it?

- A couple holding hands or the wedding rings on their fingers?

- Animals at the zoo or the people looking at them?

- A woman kneading dough or her hands covered in flour?

[ZOOM IN ON YOUR SUBJECT]

At a family gathering a while ago, my niece began dancing spontaneously (aren't kids great at that?). It was a priceless moment, so I quickly pulled out my camera to capture it on film. I wanted to get the picture before she stopped, so I took it as soon as I turned on the camera. To my delight, she kept dancing, allowing me to set up another shot—closer this time. When I got the pictures back, the difference between the two was dramatic. In the first one, my niece was only a small part of the photo amid the rest of my family members. By zooming in on her, the focus was clearly on her and her unforgettable dance.

Near subject
Photograph by Candice Stringham

 Candice's Approach:

- Step closer to your subject! Cutting the distance between you will eliminate distracting elements and put the focus on the subject.

- Create more visual interest in a close-up photo by placing the face one-third of the way into the photo instead of centering it. (This principle is called the rule of thirds; for more information, see pages 34–35.)

Far from subject
Photograph by Candice Stringham

Candice's Approach:

- Use your camera's zoom feature to take more intimate shots of your subject. If your purpose in taking the photo is to capture a facial expression, you don't need to worry about including any of the background setting.

- When taking photographs outdoors, you'll get the best pictures on cloudy days, when the sun won't produce harsh shadows on your subject's face. If the sun is shining, use your camera's fill flash to reduce the shadows. (For more information on the fill flash, see the glossary on page 102.)

With zoom
Photograph by Candice Stringham

Without zoom
Photograph by Candice Stringham

SIMILAR SITUATIONS

Zoom in close to your subject to capture these images:

- Your husband's concentration when he's working at his tool bench

- The smile of someone playing with a pet

- Your child's personality when she's talking with her friends

- The rosy cheeks of a teen who has been shoveling snow in cold temperatures

[CHANGE YOUR PERSPECTIVE]

Once my teenage growth spurt ended, I became used to seeing the world from 5'6" off the ground—5'8" when I'm wearing heels! When I pursued my love for photography, I started playing with my perspective. Climbing on a chair for a bird's-eye view, lying on the ground to capture the height of a structure—I've done it all. And my photos are all the better for it.

Photograph by Tracy White

 My Approach:

- Crouch down to your subjects' eye level to create a more intimate feeling in your photo.

- Look for lines when you take pictures—they help lead the eye through a photo. Here, the subjects' arms help guide the eye from the people to the water.

 Shannon's Approach:

- Climb to the top of the playground equipment and shoot downward so your subject is the only person in the picture even if there is a group near him.

- If you stand above your subject, make sure the sun isn't casting your shadow onto him. Try photographing on an overcast day to avoid shadows.

Photograph by Shannon Taylor

Photograph by Joy Uzarraga

Joy's Approach:

- Focus on your subjects by placing them against a simple background. If you're surrounded by bushes, homes or trees, bend down and shoot upward, using the sky as your backdrop.

- When aiming your camera toward the sky, pay attention to the location of the sun. Make sure it's not behind your subjects—it may cause them to appear as silhouettes. Instead, position your subjects so the sun is shining down on their side. Better yet, take the photo on an overcast day when the sun won't create harsh light.

- To best capture the relationship between multiple photo subjects, have them stand in natural, comfortable positions, such as with their arms around each other or looking at each other.

SIMILAR SITUATIONS

Climb on a sturdy chair or other nearby equipment and aim downward to:

- Show a child engrossed with a pile of toys on the floor

- Picture the handicraft of an artisan from his or her perspective (This works best if you stand directly behind the subject.)

- Emphasize the small stature of an infant surrounded by older children

Crouch close to the ground and look upward to:

- Capture the perspective of a basketball fan standing next to a 6'10" (or taller!) player

- Accentuate a boy's height when he's standing triumphant on a pile of dirt

Photograph a subject at eye level when you want to:

- Show the determination in her eyes as she learns to ride a bike

- Photograph the smile of a toddler when you make him laugh

[LET YOUR SUBJECTS PLAY]

When I take a picture at the beginning or end of an activity, my friends tend to notice the camera. The result? They either pose with less-than-natural smiles or back away so they're not in the shot. But when I snap my photos during the height of their activities, they're too engrossed in the event to notice my camera, allowing me to capture some great candid shots.

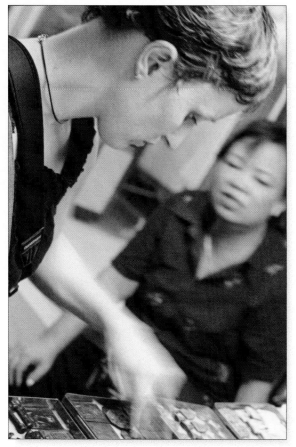

Photograph by Tracy White

 My Approach:

- When photographing a subject in motion, consider taking a shot that actually shows the action. Here, I love how the photo captures the way my friend touched every amulet at a market before making her final purchase. It shows that I photographed her in a truly natural shot, not one that's posed.

- Show movement by using a long shutter speed on your camera. (For more information on shutter speed, see the glossary on page 102.) To capture this action, use the automatic or night setting on your camera—not the action mode, which uses a fast shutter speed. (For more information on taking action photos, see Chapter 6: Action.)

Candice's Approach:

- You don't have to face your subject for every picture. If you want to take a candid shot without being noticed, you may have better luck taking the picture from the side.

- Find the direction of the subject—either horizontal or vertical—then position your camera accordingly. The line created by the boy's body and airplane in this photo made a vertical orientation the natural choice.

Photograph by Candice Stringham

Relax. Reflect. Enjoy.

SoLiTuDe.

december 2005

On Saturday mornings, Joe wakes up early and takes a bike ride around our neighborhood. He rides along the country roads while everything is still quiet and everyone is still asleep. It is his time to be alone with his thoughts. To feel the early morning chill against his face while reflecting on the past week's events. It is his chance to relax. To breathe. To rejuvenate. To appreciate everything around him. And to just be.

SOLITUDE **by Mellette Berezoski**
> Supplies *Patterned papers:* Magic Scraps and 7gypsies; *Letter stickers, molding strip and rub-ons:* Making Memories; *Metal accent:* K&Company; *Negative strip:* Narratives, Creative Imaginations; *Computer font:* GF Halda, downloaded from the Internet; *Other:* Thread and staples.

Mellette's Approach:

- Keep your camera out during activities throughout the day. Before long your subject won't pay much attention when you take a shot, allowing you to capture candid photos.

- Take advantage of your camera's zoom function. It will allow you to stand farther away from your subject, reducing the chances of being noticed when you take your shot.

- When capturing a subject in action, you'll need to anticipate his movements, then set up the shot accordingly. If you center him in the photo when you compose it, he may be moving out of it by the time the picture is actually captured. Instead, set up the shot in an area he's moving toward, so you can take the picture as he enters the frame.

SIMILAR SITUATIONS

Don't forget to capture candid shots of friends and family in these situations:

- Playing a spontaneous game of tackle football in the backyard
- Completing their homework at your kitchen table
- Enjoying a picnic at the park
- Sharing a bowl of popcorn while watching a movie together

[TELL A STORY]

If I were to tell a friend about a major event I experienced this morning, there's no way I would stop before finishing the story. It would diminish the point of telling her, and it would leave her feeling like something was missing.

I try to approach my everyday photography with the same perspective—working to capture an entire story in my pictures. And I want you to try that approach, too! Photographing the before, in-process and after shots of the happenings will help you best capture the whole story.

Photographs by Shannon Taylor

 Shannon's Approach:

- Capture the subject of the story—here, the berries—in each stage: on the bush, then picked and then stored in a jar.

- For close-up shots of your subject, use the macro setting on your camera for the most eye-catching effect.

- People are generally a part of every story, but if they're not your main focus, find creative ways to include them in your photos. In the photo showing the berries being picked, the portrait mode was used to focus on the berry (keeping it as the focus) while blurring the boy (making him a secondary subject). In the picture of the jar, hands are holding it to signify that an older man—not just the boy—participated in the activity.

"D" by Denise Pauley
> **Supplies** *Printed transparency:* K&Company; *Tab:* Autumn Leaves; *Hinges:* Making Memories; *Rubber stamp:* PSX Design; *Stamping ink:* StazOn, Tsukineko; *Pen:* Pigment Pro, American Crafts; *Computer fonts:* Times New Roman, Microsoft Word; Stamp Act, downloaded from the Internet.

 Denise's Approach:

- When photographing a child on the move, not every photo will turn out in sharp focus. Take several shots, then highlight the best ones on a layout (consider including a hidden door that opens to reveal the extra photos).

- If your subject is sitting near a wall, especially a white or light-colored wall, turn off your flash to avoid creating a silhouette on the wall (see the photos hidden in the interactive element on this page). You can also reduce the chance of silhouettes by having your subject move a couple of feet away from the wall.

- If you couldn't capture a picture of your children pulling out toys, snap a shot at the end when they're putting them away—in the finished picture, most people won't be able to tell the difference.

SIMILAR SITUATIONS

Be sure to capture multiple photos to tell these stories:
- Children decorating cookies or helping you bake a cake
- Teenagers washing their car for the first time in weeks
- The process of remodeling or reorganizing a room in your home
- Kids building a sandcastle at the park
- The progression of game pieces, play money or cards from a board game during a family activity

[WATCH FOR BACKLIT SETTINGS]

Place a flashlight behind someone and what do you see? A silhouette. In photography, that same backlit situation occurs each time there's more light behind your subject than there is between you and your subject. Avoid this by using your camera's fill flash (a flash that emits less intense light than a normal flash). Its soft light will highlight your subject's face without creating harsh shadows.

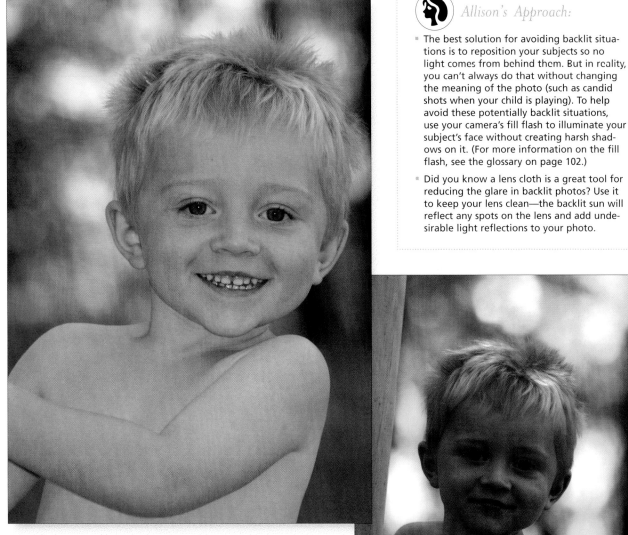

With a fill flash
Photograph by Allison Orthner

Allison's Approach:

- The best solution for avoiding backlit situations is to reposition your subjects so no light comes from behind them. But in reality, you can't always do that without changing the meaning of the photo (such as candid shots when your child is playing). To help avoid these potentially backlit situations, use your camera's fill flash to illuminate your subject's face without creating harsh shadows on it. (For more information on the fill flash, see the glossary on page 102.)

- Did you know a lens cloth is a great tool for reducing the glare in backlit photos? Use it to keep your lens clean—the backlit sun will reflect any spots on the lens and add undesirable light reflections to your photo.

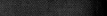
Without a fill flash

Photograph by Allison Orthner

ONE HAPPY FAMILY **by Rachel Ludwig**
> Supplies *Textured cardstock:* Bazzill Basics Paper; *Patterned paper:* Magic Scraps; *Transparency:* Autumn Leaves; *Rub-ons:* Making Memories; *Letter stickers:* Scrapworks ("Family") and American Crafts (symbols); *Rubber photo corners:* Scrapworks; *Tab:* 7gypsies; *Brads:* American Crafts; *Felt number:* Kunin Felt.

 Rachel's Approach:

- Before taking your photo, aim your camera slightly downward and let it meter away from the sun in the background. (For more information on metering, see the glossary on page 102.) Many cameras meter when you push the shutter button halfway; once it meters, continue holding it halfway, then recompose your shot to focus on the subjects and push the shutter the rest of the way to take the shot.

- Take a "family portrait" that focuses on the child by placing him a few feet in front of his parents. Bend down to his level and compose the shot in portrait mode to create a nice depth of field.

SIMILAR SITUATIONS

You'll find backlit situations both indoors and outdoors. Pay particular attention to this type of lighting when photographing:

- A family positioned on a couch below a window
- Friends outside facing away from the sun on a sunny day
- Someone in front of a mirror or a picture frame (covered with glass) when you use your camera's flash (The light from the flash will bounce off the glass and fill the space behind your subject.)
- Adults standing in front of or near an indoor light

chapter 2 # portraits

QUICK: NAME THE MOST VALUABLE TREASURE IN YOUR LIFE. What was the first thing that came to mind? I'd be willing to guess it was a person— or multiple people. That's because relationships are so priceless. Chances are, the people around you are the reason you started taking pictures in the first place. (If you have a child, you probably can't even count the number of pictures you took during her first few months of life!)

That's why capturing good photographs of family and friends is so important. We want to remember who these people are at each stage of their lives. And we want to make sure the portraits we take are ones they're going to love. After all, aren't we all self-conscious about how we look in photos? I am. By practicing some tips for taking portraits, you can help your subjects feel comfortable when you photograph them and assure them they'll love the results. The best part is that you'll have unforgettable pictures that you and those close to you will treasure for generations.

P.S. For tips on photographing babies, children, teens and adults specifi-cally, check out the ideas in the appendix, pages 103–113.

While shopping one day, I found a tiled vase I absolutely loved. The light that shone through the store window made its colors reflect brilliantly. I couldn't resist, so I purchased it and took it home. I placed it on a table in my office that night, but it didn't look the same. I admit, I was a little disappointed.

When I entered my office the next day, the vase had regained its colorful nature. The difference? It was daytime, so the sun was shining through my window. The natural light reflecting on the side of the vase helped capture its colors, picking up the details of each tile.

Photograph by Elizabeth Ruuska

 Elizabeth's Approach:

- Place your subject near a window so the light comes in from the side. Just make sure the sun isn't beaming directly through the window—you want the light to be reflected inside for a softer look. If you can see the sun through your window, its light can produce harsh shadows on your subject's face.

- A large window will provide more light, though an average-sized window is sufficient for head-and-shoulder portraits.

- Bold hats can draw attention away from a face. To keep the focus on the face, balance the hat with another accent, such as a necklace, that adds balance to the colors in the photo.

Candice's Approach:

- North-facing windows are the most reliable source of natural light because the sun will never shine directly through them—all the light is reflected, making it softer and more flattering in pictures.

- Avoid clothing with writing or bold designs—they'll draw attention away from your subject's face.

- If you're photographing your subject from above, have her wear a soft-colored shirt—the color will add warmth to the photo without drawing attention away from her face.

Photograph by Candice Stringham

PURE JOY **by Shannon Montez**
> Supplies *Patterned paper and epoxy stickers:* MOD, Autumn Leaves; *Computer font:* Carpenter, downloaded from the Internet.

Shannon's Approach:

- While it's best to use north-facing windows, that may not always be possible. If your child happens to flash a funny face near a window without optimum light, take the shot anyway. If you notice harsh shadows across the face, use your camera's fill flash to soften them.

- East-facing windows can actually add a beautiful warm glow to your photos in the evening, when the sun is setting and its light reflects into your home. (Likewise, west-facing windows can create nice side lighting in early morning hours.)

SIMILAR SITUATIONS

Don't have any large north-facing windows in your home? Try these ideas for achieving side lighting:

- Open your garage door and let the light shine in. (Simply drape a sheet behind your subject for a nice backdrop.) On a sunny day, when the sun is reflecting off the driveway or sidewalk, the light reflects inside; reflected light is much prettier than direct sunlight.

- Take an outside shot under a covered porch. Again, this is best on a bright, sunny day when the sunlight is reflecting off the sidewalk. On a cloudy day, the photos may appear too dark.

- If you don't have a north-facing window in your home, watch the light in your environment. Maybe the sunlight hits the home next to yours—that light will reflect into your house. In fact, the northern windows in my home are in small rooms that don't have much space for a photo shoot. I've never taken a photo in those rooms. Instead, I take photos in my living room with east-facing windows and a small southern window that's close to the ceiling.

[FOLLOW THE RULE OF THIRDS]

Learning about the "rule of thirds" changed the way I composed my photographs. I usually placed my subject's face in the center of my frame, but the result undoubtedly looked flat. I tried using the rule of thirds, and my photos looked dramatically different.

What is the rule of thirds? It's a simple principle that artists have been using for centuries.

When you look through your viewfinder, think of imaginary lines dividing the picture into thirds horizontally and vertically (see the diagram at below). Then, place your subject at a point where two of the lines intersect. By envisioning these lines and using them in your photograph, you create a ratio of 2:1 in your photo, making the composition look stable and intriguing rather than static.

Photograph by Rhonda Stark

 *Rhonda's Approach:*

- Take advantage of multiple lines in a single photo—this picture uses both a horizontal and a vertical line.

- If your subject is looking directly into the camera, center the intersecting point between her eyes.

- You can position brightly colored items along the one-third lines to enhance the effect of the rule of thirds. In this shot, the pink camisole and the pink flip-flop are positioned nicely along an envisioned vertical and horizontal line, respectively.

Nichol's Approach:

- When deciding which envisioned line to use as you photograph your subject, pay attention to the direction of his body. Here, the body is facing toward the right side of the picture frame, so the head was positioned along the left-hand line. Having the subject face into the photo creates a warmer, more intimate feeling.

- If you position your subject near a window, place him at a diagonal to the light so it falls gently across the side of his face.

Photograph by Nichol Magouirk

Photograph by Candice Stringham

Candice's Approach:

- For extreme close-up shots, center your subject's head along an envisioned vertical line.
- Add a dramatic flair to your picture by positioning your subject's body facing away from the photo (here, the man is facing right and is placed on the right-hand envisioned vertical line).

SIMILAR SITUATIONS

You'll be able to use the rule of thirds for almost any photo, such as:

- Landscape photos of a sunset. Place the horizon along one of the horizontal lines.
- Pictures of historic buildings. Center the building along a vertical line.
- Shots of a friend ice-skating on a lake. When she's skating to the right, capture her in the top-left intersection point.
- Candid pictures of a child gazing at a hot-air balloon. Capture your child near the bottom-right intersection point and the balloon centered in the top-left one.

[FOCUS ON PERSONALITY]

When I look at my childhood portraits, I wonder how anyone who looked at them knew what I was like. Each one looks like a school portrait—I'm sitting up straight and only my shoulders and head are showing. You don't see that I loved to sing, that I lit up whenever I held a kitty, or that I couldn't stop giggling when I tackled my dad and tickled his toes.

Since I don't want my subjects to look like static people in their portraits, I make sure to pinpoint a part of their personality, then attempt to capture that emotion when I take the photographs.

Photograph by Tracy White

 My Approach:

- Does your subject have a favorite outfit, one she knows she looks great in? Have her wear it. She'll feel more confident, which means she'll be more at ease in letting her personality show.

- Introduce an animal into the picture. When your subject starts to play with him, you'll see her personality in a more natural setting.

 Rhonda's Approach:

- Want to see your subject's face light up? Simply make her laugh!

- Your subject doesn't necessarily have to stand for a full-body shot. By having her sit, you can capture her entire body without creating a lot of empty space on the sides of the photo.

- Chairs create nice props that add a simple contrast to a solid-colored background. They also allow your subject to relax—a key in getting great personality shots.

Photograph by Rhonda Stark

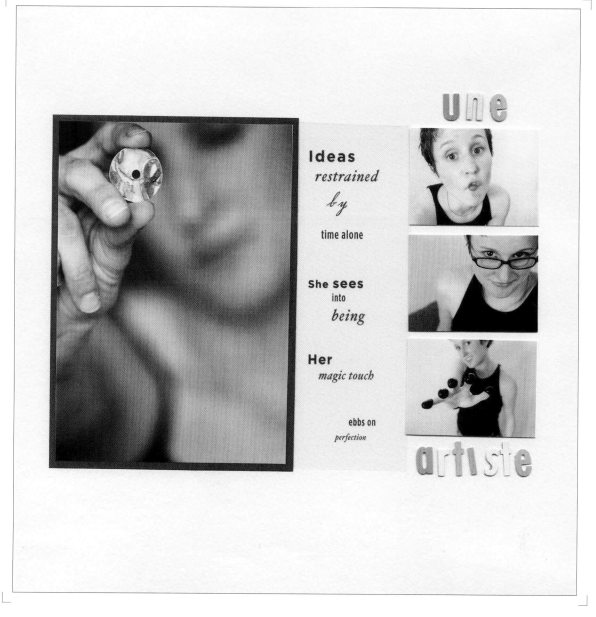

UNE ARTISTE **by Tracy White**
> **Supplies** *Metal letters:* KI Memories; *Computer fonts:* Gotham, Hoefler Italic Swash and Dear Sarah, downloaded from the Internet.

 *My Approach:*

- Photographing a close friend? Ham it up along with her! When the two of you laugh like you would on any other day, you'll be able to capture some memorable portraits.

- Does your subject have a hobby? Capture that aspect of her personality. In the enlarged photo on this page, the focus is on the jewelry the subject made while her face is blurred in the background.

SIMILAR SITUATIONS

Keep these additional ideas in mind when you're capturing personality:

- Have your subject tell you a story, whether it's her most embarrassing moment or her favorite memory from the past week. Have your camera ready—her personality is sure to come through when she talks.

- Bring a child into the room and everyone goes gaga. If you or your subject have a small child, have them play together to put her in a joyful mood.

- Photographing an athlete? Head out to the field where she feels at home.

[DETERMINE THE DISTANCE]

Whenever I'm with friends and ask a stranger to take a photo of us, I specify how close I want the shot to be (a close-up picture of our faces or a full-body shot that captures a building in the background). If I forget to mention it, the photos are undoubtedly taken from far away, often when the background is unnecessary. Sure, I can always crop out the background later, but selecting the best distance for each photo ahead of time creates a much better result.

 Candice's Approach:

- A full-length portrait is great for documenting a subject's body characteristics. But unless the background is truly exciting, the result may be lackluster because of the dead space on the sides of the photo. Make the photo more dramatic by having the person dress in an eye-catching outfit or including unique props that draw viewers' attention. (You don't normally see a kitchen chair in an alleyway, so it makes you take a second look at this photo.)

- Pictures showing just the head, shoulders and torso (three-quarters shots) can help a shy photo subject feel more comfortable than an extreme close-up shot will, because the camera is farther away from him. To add more interest to the photo, blur the background while keeping the subject and foreground in focus.

- As you zoom in, make sure you don't visually cut off the arms at an odd location, such as at the elbow or the shoulder. If your subject is wearing short sleeves, avoid framing the edge of the photo just beyond the end of the sleeves (it will create a tangent in the photo that leads the eye away from the subject's face).

Full-body shot
Three-quarters shot
Head shot
Photographs by
Candice Stringham

Before
Photograph by Candice Stringham

After
Photograph by Candice Stringham

[EXPERIMENT OUTSIDE]

I once set up a photo shoot for my neighbor's toddler. I'd positioned her near a window and even had toys to entertain her between shots. After several attempts, I still hadn't captured her personality like I wanted. I wondered if it was that her two-year-old attention span kept her from enjoying the picture-taking process. Then her mom said, "She probably wants to go outside and play," and it hit me: she's just not an indoor girl—she'd prefer to be outside at any time of the day. To truly photograph her personality, I needed to set up the shoot outside. Out we went. Once she was in her element, it was easy to take the shots I hoped for.

Before
Photograph by Candice Stringham

After
Photograph by Candice Stringham

 Candice's Approach:

- These shots were taken outside on a sunny day; however, no harsh shadows appear on the subject's face because he's positioned next to a wall that blocks the sun (the sun is on the east side of the building, and the subject is on the west side).

- When taking portraits, pay attention to a person's joints. Make sure you don't crop an arm or a leg out of the photo at these spots—step back or get closer if needed to change the composition. In the before photo, the edges of the photo cut off the man's left arm and right knee. In the after photo, there's no odd cropping.

- When deciding how far to zoom in on your subject, decide what story you want to tell in the picture, then crop in far enough to keep only the pertinent details and eliminate the rest. (This range will change for every photo.)

Photograph by Candice Stringham

 Candice's Approach:

- Outdoor portraits are best taken on cloudy days, when the light is softer and less likely to cast harsh shadows on your subject's face. If you can't avoid a sunny day, bring a reflector, such as a white poster board, and place it opposite the light source to soften the shadows. In this picture, the reflector was placed on the lower-left side of the photo since the sun is shining from the upper-right side.

- If you want to focus on your subject, select a simple background for the photo, such as a solid-colored wall. In this photo, the red barn even coordinates with the boy's shirt.

SIMILAR SITUATIONS

Try these other solutions if you photograph out-doors on a sunny day:

- Position your subject under a large tree so the leaves block the direct sun and reduce shadows. But watch for dappled lighting where leaves are sparse, as it can create odd shadows.

- If you're photographing a small child, bring along another adult. Have him or her stand between the child and the sun. *Note:* This will only work for head shots. In full-body shots, there won't be enough coverage, and you'll be able to see the adult's shadow on the ground.

- Use your camera's fill flash, which provides less-intense light that illuminates dark spots without creating harsh shadows of its own.)For more information on the fill flash, see the glossary on page 102.)

Ah, "family photo time." Doesn't always bring the most joyful thoughts, does it? (I imagine picking out matching outfits and trying to keep my nieces and nephews still—and I've got 14 of them!) But it doesn't have to be that way. I remember one year as a child when my family decided to forego the professional route and have my brother—a budding photographer—take the annual photo (he used a tripod to set up the photo, then used the self-timer and ran into position). We all felt more comfortable, and we could really be ourselves. We loved the results—they had a way of speaking to us. We decided to set up these shoots more often!

Photograph by Becky Higgins

Candice's Approach:

- Not all group photos have to be shots of people's faces—capturing your subjects from behind during a simple stroll can add a unique perspective to the picture.

- When photographing little children with an adult, make sure you include an interesting background so the photo isn't filled with empty white space.

- Group photos don't have to be posed. If you see an opportunity for a great shot (no matter where you are), take it.

Becky's Approach:

- Arrange your subjects' faces so they form an oval—this composition helps lead the eye naturally through every face in the picture. You'll achieve a similar effect when the faces form a visual triangle.

- Look for soft, natural lighting, like that on a cloudy day. With so many faces in the picture, you're bound to notice shadows if the lighting is harsh.

- Does someone in the group wear glasses? Have him lift the frames slightly behind his ears. You won't notice the tilt in the picture, but it will prevent the lenses from reflecting light.

- Encourage your subjects to pose naturally. Have them place their arms around each other or lean together. Just make sure they're comfortable so they feel (and look) like themselves.

Photograph by Candice Stringham

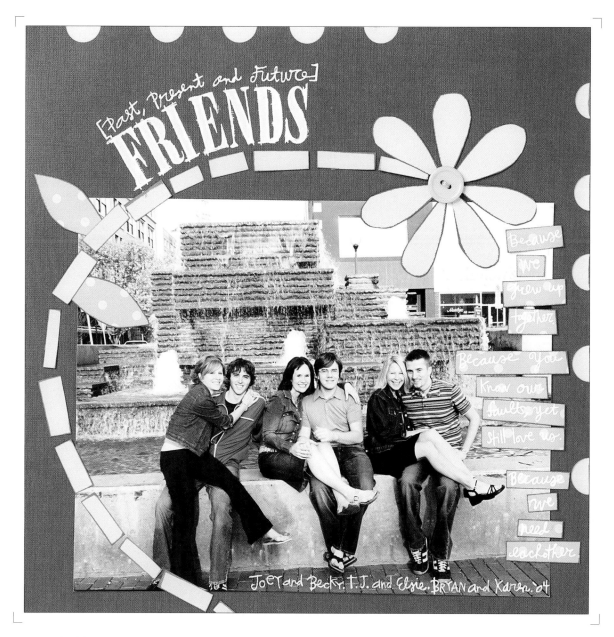

FRIENDS **by Elsie Flannigan**
> Supplies *Textured cardstock:* Bazzill Basics Paper; *Patterned papers:* Chatterbox and Making Memories; *Rub-ons:* Making Memories; *Punch:* EK Success; *Acrylic paint:* Heidi Swapp for Advantus; *Stamping ink:* ColorBox, Clearsnap; *White pen:* Uni-ball, Sanford; *Other:* Button and thread.

Elsie's Approach:

- Take a lot of photos! Professionals don't stop after one photo, and neither should you. The more photos you take, the greater your chances of getting a photo where no one is blinking and everyone is looking at the camera.

- When applying the rule of thirds (for more information, see page 34–35) to a group setting, focus on the horizontal lines, rather than the intersecting points. *Note:* If your subjects are positioned in two rows, let faces on the back row align with the top horizontal line and faces on the front row align with the bottom horizontal line.

- Look for objects that fill in white space while complementing your photo. Here, the lines on the waterfall structure complement the line of subjects.

SIMILAR SITUATIONS

To enhance your group photos, consider these ideas:

- Find a piece of furniture your subjects can gather around—a piano bench or some chairs work well.

- Does the family have a nice backyard? Take some shots in it for a personalized photo.

- Head to a nearby park. Have your subjects sit on the ground and let the grassy fields in the background set the backdrop.

- If your subjects are sitting or kneeling, remember to crouch close to the ground as well.

chapter 3 your
environment

WHEN PEOPLE ASK MY NEIGHBORS WHERE THEY LIVE, THEY PROBABLY

reply, "In the city." To me, it's much more than that. It's living in an

early-twentieth-century home that carries with it reminders of an earlier

time. It's having a porch that draws me outside rather than air

conditioning that pushes me indoors. It's driving down streets with old

and new buildings that speak volumes about the people who built the

magnificent architecture.

In short, it's about the details.

What does your environment say about you? More importantly, what can

you say—in pictures—about your environment? The way you compose

each photograph you take of your surroundings reflects the way you feel

about the buildings and objects that make up your life, whether you're

at home, in the city or even on vacation. How can you best capture these

details? I'll share some of my favorite tips in this chapter.

[CAPTURE DETAILS OF HOME]

My home says a lot about me. It's filled with treasures I've picked up during my travels—from the old Buddha I bought in Bangkok to the charcoal drawings I purchased in Paris. These details reveal the adventurous aspect of my personality. (They also provide interesting objects for exploring and refining my still-life photography skills!) I know that without taking pictures of these items, I wouldn't be leaving a complete story of my life when future generations look through my scrapbooks.

Photograph by Becky Higgins

 Becky's Approach:

- Play with composition to get the most out of your photographs. Instead of just taking a picture of your bookshelves, try to capture the chair where you love to read those books in the same shot.

- If you include two objects in your picture, decide which is more important to you. Then, focus on that item while letting the other item blur. If you want to highlight the object in front, simply use the portrait mode. If you want to focus on the item in the background, move your camera to focus on it. On most cameras, you'll need to press the shutter button halfway down. Once it has focused, continue holding the button halfway down, then move your camera back to your original composition. (For more information on creating depth of field, see the glossary on page 102.)

 Annie's Approach:

- When taking pictures at home, you can select the best lighting conditions for your photos since you can set up the shot any time. Add a soft glow to the shot by taking it during early morning hours.

- Tell a story with your detail shots. Like to read the morning paper on your patio while enjoying a sweet orange? Capture your haven on film!

Photograph by Annie Weis

MY FAVORITE BOUQUET **by Rhonda Stark**
> **Supplies** *Software:* Adobe Photoshop CS, Adobe Systems; *Patterned papers and date stamp:* DesignerDigitals.com; *Computer fonts:* AL Verdigris, "15 Vintage Fonts" CD, Autumn Leaves; Shortcut, downloaded from *www.dafont.com*; TIA Pick-Me-Up, downloaded from *www.DesignerDigitals.com*.

Rhonda's Approach:

- You don't always need to clear away the table to photograph a floral arrangement without a distracting background. Sometimes a little contrast adds interest—just blur the background by using the portrait mode to keep the focus on the flowers. If you have an SLR camera, you can create the same effect with a fast shutter speed and wide aperture.

- Remember to turn off the flash and use natural lighting—it will prevent harsh shadows from appearing on your object. If you need to use the flash (for example, if you're photographing an object in a room without natural light), pay attention to your camera's flash range so you don't end up with a "blown out" photograph that looks overexposed.

- Photograph the object from multiple angles, then combine two of the pictures on a layout for a creative touch.

SIMILAR SITUATIONS

Look around your home and take pictures that reveal who you are, such as detail shots of:

- Your favorite books
- The most-used items in each room
- An inside view of your refrigerator
- Your closet
- The furniture in your living room
- Shoes in your mudroom or garage
- Blankets and pillows on your bed

[FIND PATTERNS]

A few years ago, I planted a flower garden in front of my home. After I planted the first flower, my phone rang, so I stopped to answer it. While I was talking, I looked at the garden and couldn't help but think how empty it looked with only one flower in it. It wouldn't have made for a very exciting picture. When I finished planting the remaining flowers, the result was completely different. The line of flowers created a focal point for the garden—and for an eye-catching photo. Why? Because the eye is drawn to repetition—to patterns. When you look for them in the subjects you photograph, you'll be able to capture that same rhythm in your pictures.

Photograph by Tracy White

📷 *My Approach:*

- If you want to include an object in your photo that isn't the same shape as the items around it, think creatively. By walking around the pile of green vegetables and using it to frame the bottom of the photo, I implied a round shape that mimicked the rest of the pots.

- For better visual balance, place "heavy" or larger objects near the bottom of your picture and smaller items near the top.

- Traveling through a covered market? Look for side lighting near the edge of the overhead covering to enhance the pictures.

 ## *My Approach:*

- This photo incorporates two patterns: lines (from the tools) and circles (from the handle ends and the large dish).

- Notice how the tools point to the top-center section of the photo? Had they faced downward, they would have led the eye off the bottom of the photo. I walked around the table so the tools were facing upward, establishing a composition that draws the eye into the photograph instead of away from it.

Photograph by Tracy White

AUSTRALIA **by Jamie Waters**
> **Supplies** *Patterned paper:* American Crafts; *Chipboard phrase, title lettering and metal ring:* Li'l Davis Designs.

Jamie's Approach:

- A photo with stairs and pillars adds contrast because of the perpendicular lines they create. For the most effective shot, walk down the stairs and shoot upward.

- Heading to a popular site? Wake up early and arrive before anyone else so you don't have people in the background of your photos. You'll also be able to utilize the nice morning light.

SIMILAR SITUATIONS

Look for patterns in these objects as well:

- Bikes lined along a wall at the park
- A row of books in an office
- Boats docked in a harbor
- Shops along a market street (Photograph them from one side rather than from the front for a more intriguing effect.)
- Tubes of paint lying near a palette
- Street lamps (During the day they form "I" patterns; in the early morning and late afternoon hours, when their shadows are long, they create "L" patterns.)

[LOOK FOR FRAMES]

I would never think about hanging a photo on my wall without putting it in a frame—it would get lost on the expanse of my wall. Since the picture itself would have hardly any depth, there would be nothing to draw my eye to it. But the moment I put a photo in a frame and hang it up, the picture quickly becomes a focal point of the room.

Next time you're taking a picture of your environment, try creating a frame within your photo, something that will draw viewers' eyes to the subject. See that doorframe? It provides a natural frame for the subject behind it. Notice a tree growing over a park bench? It's a great frame for a photo, too.

 My Approach:

- It's natural to walk through a doorway to avoid having it in the photograph. Instead, step behind it and include it as a frame for the photo.
- Position your subject in the center of two converging lines and the eye is quickly drawn toward her.
- A frame doesn't have to cover all four sides of a picture. It can fill one, two or three edges of the photo and still look nice.

 Sande's Approach:

- You don't have to look for natural objects surrounding your subjects—have them stand behind or lean through a manmade frame, such as the tire in this shot. The center of the tire naturally draws the eye toward the boys.
- If you want to draw extra attention to a particular photo subject, position him in the point of greatest light in the picture. Notice how the boy in the sun draws more attention than the boy in the shade?
- To avoid harsh lines created on sunny days, as in this photo, use your camera's fill flash for a softer look.

Photograph by Tracy White

Photograph by Sande Krieger

Photograph by Sande Krieger

 Sande's Approach:

- Don't forget to look up for frames as well! By having subjects climb stairs, you can utilize the railings for a unique photo frame.

- Tungsten lights (the ones most commonly used in homes) will cast an orange glow over your photo. To avoid this, buy specialty film or filters designed for tungsten lighting. If you have a digital camera, see if your camera has a setting that automatically compensates for it. When possible, use natural light instead.

[PAY ATTENTION TO LIGHT]

You know what I love about the rain? The way it falls on the ground and reflects the lights on my street at night. Can't you just picture the way it lights up your street at night? It's a beautiful phenomenon. Using reflected light will work wonders in your photos as well—just remember to keep these tips in mind.

Photograph by Brenda Arnall

Brenda's Approach:

- Without the correct metering, the subject in your photo may look like either a giant ball of light (called "floodlighting") or a small star against a large black background. Zoom in until your subject fills the frame—it will allow the camera to meter correctly and will capture the scene in more detail.

- Night shots are best taken 30 to 40 minutes after the sun sets. The sky is dark enough to show lights, but there's a lingering glow that will prevent the background of your photo from looking jet black.

Sande's Approach:

- You'll find warm lighting away from water as well. Pay attention to luminaries, candelabras and more to find some great shots.

- Before composing your photograph, look around at the setting. Is one luminary darker than the rest? If so, use it as your focal point when you take the picture—when both the foreground and background are filled with light, this focal point will help the camera determine the best metering for the shot.

Photograph by Sande Krieger

"Mom...wait!" The urgency in Spencer's voice made me hesitate. He had been a good sport, letting me drag him out of bed every morning around 5 am to go out and shoot pictures. In my opinion, that's the only way to see Venice...sans people. Sure, there are a few people moving around at that hour, like the baker in the window across from our apartment. Every morning we awoke to the mouth watering smells of pastries he was making to sell in his little shop below. I turned to looked up the alley where Spencer was pointing. Even at the young age of 12, he has an eye for photographic composition. When I looked at Venice through his eyes, she was even more beautiful than I remembered.

October 2004

VENEZIA THROUGH SPENCER'S EYES **by Sande Krieger**
> **Supplies** *Photo paper:* Epson; *Textured cardstock:* Bazzill Basics Paper and unknown; *Flower and brad:* Nunn Design; *Software:* Adobe Photoshop CS, Adobe Systems; *Computer fonts:* Monotype Corsiva (journaling), Microsoft Word; Adobe Jensen Pro ("Through Spencer's Eyes"), Adobe Systems.

Sande's Approach:

- When you're capturing reflections at night, it's imperative to use your tripod. You need the actual object to appear completely in focus so it creates a contrast with the blurred, reflected image in the water.

- Mix candlelight and water and the result is always stunning—the candles add a rich, warm glow to the photo.

- Reflections photographed under a bridge create a visual mind game because there's no horizon line to present a clear point of reflection. The effect is sure to make viewers take a second look at the photo to decipher the image.

SIMILAR SITUATIONS

Be sure to watch for floodlighting when you photograph:

- A street at night after a rainstorm
- Garden parties near a swimming pool
- Close-up detail shots on buildings lit by spotlights at night (even when there's no water near)

[EXPLORE NONTRADITIONAL VIEWS]

Wherever I travel, I love to snap pictures at the "tourist stops." They always make for great shots, but they look like every other photo or postcard of the tourist attractions. So once I make my "tourist stops," I continue looking for my own "photographer stops"—places where I can capture the same tourist locations in a unique way. When I capture these photographs, I feel like a true artist.

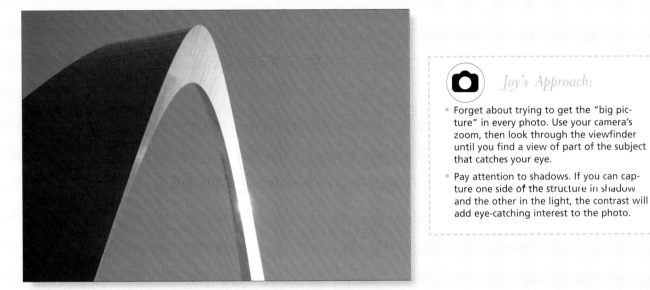

Photograph by Joy Uzarraga

Joy's Approach:

- Forget about trying to get the "big picture" in every photo. Use your camera's zoom, then look through the viewfinder until you find a view of part of the subject that catches your eye.

- Pay attention to shadows. If you can capture one side of the structure in shadow and the other in the light, the contrast will add eye-catching interest to the photo.

Annie's Approach:

- Did you spend more time looking at a memorable site from your car than on foot? Tell the story in your picture by photographing your subject with the car framing it.

- If you take photos while moving in the car, use the action mode on your camera to reduce the chance of blurring.

- Traveling alone? Set your camera on the dash of your car and use the self-timer to snap a portrait of yourself.

Photograph by Annie Weis

Only crumbling remnants remain to hint of past glory.
12th century elegance defeated by 17th century strength.
Unique alcoves designed for arrows and crossbows.
A hilltop, double moat with bridges and panoramic view.
The chance to explore the present and imagine the past.
Helmsley Castle
England May 2004
regal ruins

REGAL RUINS **by Brenda Arnall**

> **Supplies** *Textured cardstock:* Bazzill Basics Paper; *Patterned papers:* Deluxe Designs (purple), SEI (green) and Sticker Studio ("passport"); *Rub-ons:* Chatterbox; *Ribbon, charm, photo turn, brads and metal letters:* Making Memories; *Tab:* 7gypsies; *Stamping ink:* ColorBox, Clearsnap; *Pens:* Pigment Pro, American Crafts; *Computer font:* Butterbrotpapier, downloaded from the Internet.

Brenda's Approach:

- To best tell the story of a building, take several photos of it from different locations. With multiple perspectives, your photos will say much more than any postcard shot could.
- At a historical site? Find a way to capture the way earlier residents would have viewed the structure, such as taking a photo from the inside looking out.
- Did you notice the frames created in these pictures? All four of them use a frame!

SIMILAR SITUATIONS

As you walk around a structure, consider taking photos from these locations:

- Stand directly underneath a monument and look up
- Head for higher ground, then snap the photo from above
- If a lake borders one side of the building, drive to the other side of it and use a telephoto lens to capture the structure
- Walk one hundred feet or more to the side of the structure and compose a shot—you'll usually find more intriguing lines there
- If your child is sitting on your shoulders to get a better view, hand her the camera and have her take the picture

[CAPTURE THE NIGHT LIFE]

Green acres is not the place for me—I much prefer the city life. It's amazing to think that thousands of people surround me, each with their own story. I love talking with them in stores and at concerts, learning a bit of the rich history that fills our cities. So when I see a skyscraper, I wonder what story each person in that building has to share. While I'll never be able to talk with each individual, I like to take a picture of the skyline and think about everything there is to uncover in the city.

Photograph by Tracy White

 My Approach:

- To capture the height of multiple buildings in a skyline, it's important to photograph them from a distance. Driving a few minutes away will create a better picture.

- Create a longer depth of field in your photo by including an object up close in the foreground. Here, the emphasis is on the water, making the buildings look farther away.

- Your shutter will remain open longer at night, so it's important to avoid camera shake. Place your camera on a wall or tripod and use the self-timer.

My Approach:

- Cities are filled with interesting images at night. Keep your eyes open as you drive and you'll find several objects worth photographing.

- Night shots are often difficult to meter. When possible, let the lit objects fill your frame so the camera has more light to meter. Here, I positioned the bridge in the top third of the photo instead of the bottom third, because the water reflected extra light while the sky did not.

Photograph by Tracy White

Photograph by Annie Weis

Annie's Approach:

- Cityscapes look beautiful when set against a glowing sunset. You'll need to arrive at your destination well before the sun sets to make sure your shot is set up when the sun actually goes down—the best colors pass quickly.

- Instead of capturing the height of a skyline, photograph the city with a bird's-eye view. Simply find a tall building and head to the top or drive into the mountains if you live near them.

- If you're taking photos inside a building, be sure to turn off your flash so it doesn't reflect off the window. (The scene is too far away for the flash to be effective anyway.)

SIMILAR SITUATIONS

Consider taking these additional night shots you'll find in the city:

- Neon signs that illuminate store fronts

- Cars speeding along a highway (Find a high location, then use a long shutter speed to capture the movement.)

- Street lights creating interesting patterns along a road

- Marquee lights highlighting a theater sign

chapter 4 # nature and landscape

LIVING IN UTAH, I'M BLESSED TO HAVE BREATHTAKING MOUNTAINS SET the backdrop for my day-to-day life. I love seeing them blanketed with snow in the winter, covered with green trees in the summer, and bursting with red, orange and yellow leaves during autumn.

But you know what? Sometimes I forget how amazing they are because I see them every day. In fact, last fall I was so preoccupied with my work responsibilities and personal errands that the leaves had been changing for a full week before I even stopped to take a good look at them. If just once in those seven days I had pulled to the side of the road and taken a moment to truly look at them through my car window, I would have seen the picture-perfect setting for some great fall shots. I even had my camera with me! I'd simply forgotten to pause and notice the changing environment surrounding me.

No matter where you live, the world around you is filled with amazing images. From your neighborhood to your city to distant scenes, you'll see eye-catching designs everywhere—if you look.

[LOOK FOR LINES]

When I look through my scrapbook pages, I quickly notice a trend—the use of lines. Yep, they're everywhere. Why? Because they lead the eye through the page, from the photos to the journaling and the accents. This same principle is prevalent in my pictures as well. Lines have a strong visual power I can use to lead a viewer's eye to a particular point of interest in the picture or to help catch his or her attention.

Photograph by Candice Stringham

 Candice's Approach:

- The horizon creates a natural horizontal line in nearly every nature photograph. No matter where you go, you'll always see the horizon, so it's a reliable starting point for your lines.

- If your setting is an open expanse where the horizon is the only line, add contrast (and interest) by having someone stand in the photo to create a perpendicular line.

- In early morning and evening hours, the sun lies closer to the horizon, casting longer shadows on your photo subjects. Photograph during these times if you plan to create lines with shadows.

Joy's Approach:

- Lines created by objects closer to the camera appear more dominant than those in the background. In this photo, the tree near the right edge of the frame is the closest, making its trunk appear wider than the trunks of the other trees and drawing extra attention to it.

- To keep the focus on the field instead of on the dominant vertical line of the nearest tree, place another vertical subject (here, the boy) on the opposite side of the picture for balance.

- Lines add a sense of stability to photos. Young children running tend to look unstable, but including lines in the photo can counter that.

Photograph by Joy Uzarraga

Brenda's Approach:

- Lines won't always be obvious, like they are with the horizon, but if you look closely, you'll find them in almost any scene. The key is to keep your eyes open as you prepare to take your photo, then build your composition around the lines.

- This photo is filled with lines—the line of the three birds, the lines of each bird's wingspan, the line created by the bird's shadows and the line formed by the wake the birds left. All of these lines ensure that the eye is naturally drawn toward the birds in the foreground.

- Lines imply a sense of action. Notice the wake line moving from the left side of the photo to the right? It lets you know the birds are moving toward the right.

- If you want an above-average shot, you'll need to make an above-average effort. This shot wouldn't have been the same if taken from the seashore instead of from a boat on the water.

Photograph by Brenda Arnall

Shannon's Approach:

- Vertical lines show movement, such as the feeling that the water flows downstream in this picture.

- Converging lines (two lines that appear to be approaching each other in the distance) create a sense of depth in a photograph. Placing an object in the front of the picture exaggerates this distance, making the stream look even more distant in the background.

- Draw attention to your photo subject by centering him between converging lines—they'll naturally move the eye toward him.

SIMILAR SITUATIONS

Manmade items can also create lines in your landscape photos. Here are a few ideas:

- A picket fence in front of a pasture
- Train tracks crossing through a field
- Stone walls backing a row of hedges
- Buildings lining the sides of a street leading toward the ocean

Photograph by Shannon Taylor

[THINK ABOUT SCALE]

Last year I had a chance to climb the Sydney Harbour Bridge. Before I started my climb, the bridge seemed so large. Once I reached the top, however, the bridge didn't look large anymore; instead, the scenery below looked small. Of course, the landscape didn't change—just my perspective on it. I love that part of nature photography. Simply changing my position or frame composition lets me control the way the land looks in my finished photo.

Photograph by Tracy White

 My Approach:

- Want to emphasize the distance of a background object? Include a close-up object (the fence here) in the foreground. Since the closer item will appear larger, it will make the background scene seem smaller (and smaller objects give the feeling of greater distance).

- Minimize the height of a hill by finding higher ground from which to take your photo.

 Annie's Approach:

- People are great tools for emphasizing the size of your landscape. The eye knows how large a person should be, so he or she provides a good reference point when determining scale in the photo.

- Make a foreground look more massive by having subjects stand far from the camera in the background of the photo. Since the people look small, the foreground appears larger.

- Crouch low to the ground to emphasize the objects in the foreground.

Photograph by Annie Weis

Photograph by Shannon Taylor

 Shannon's Approach:

- Emphasize the distance between a foreground subject and background landscape by photographing your subject in the sunlight and the background in shadow.

- Have your photo subject face into the picture (not toward the camera, but toward the scene you're photographing). Viewers will follow his gaze, keeping their eyes in the photo.

- If possible, photograph landscapes when the sun is shining to the side of you. When the sun is directly behind you, shadows will disappear behind the landscape, making the objects look flat. If the sun is facing you, the photo may become backlit, leaving only silhouettes of the landscape.

SIMILAR SITUATIONS

You can emphasize the size of:
- Mountains when you crouch low to the ground and aim upward
- Rivers by bending near them along the bank and shooting upstream
- Trees when you lie down near the base and take the photo directly toward the sky
- Flowers by placing your camera on the ground and using the self-timer to take the picture

You can minimize the size of:
- Mountains and rivers by finding a nearby hill and standing on it to take your picture
- Trees when someone stands near you in the foreground of the photo and the trees are a good distance away
- Flowers by standing directly above them and looking downward

[CONSIDER THE SEASON]

While some people may love living in a warm, paradise-like climate year round, I prefer experiencing the changing seasons. Each one presents new opportunities for developing my photography skills. The key is exploration—determining which colors work best with snow or finding the perfect composition for photographing a spring tulip. I encourage you to play with the possibilities each season presents. Let these tips get you started.

Photograph by Sande Krieger

 Sande's Approach:

- Most fall pictures are taken to showcase several colors together. For a unique approach, select a monochromatic color scheme for your photo. Notice how the leaf, skin, hair and background in this shot come from the same color family?

- If you want to include a photo subject but maintain focus on a seasonal object, make it seem larger than it is, such as the leaf in this picture. Have the photo subject hold the object as far away from her as possible, or even hold it yourself while she stands farther back.

 Sande's Approach:

- Tree branches covered with snow create great photo ops for winter. (Photos with color amid the snow will have more appeal than photos filled only with white snow.)

- To capture frost or light snowfalls, you'll need to head outside early in the morning. The later in the day you take the shot, the more snow will have melted.

Photograph by Sande Krieger

NATURE IS THE ART OF GOD **by Shelley Laming**
> **Supplies** *Patterned papers:* Anna Griffin, Paperfever and Scrapworks; *Transparency:* 7gypsies; *Die-cut accent:* Heidi Swapp for Advantus; *Stamping ink:* ColorBox, Clearsnap; *Pen:* Zig Writer, EK Success; *Other:* Staples.

Shelley's Approach:

- Don't be afraid to get a little dirty—lie down near your flower bed and photograph a flower at its height.

- If multiple flower buds fill your photo, position the most dominant one according to the rule of thirds: envision vertical and horizontal lines dividing your picture into nine equal boxes, then place the flower over the inside corner of one box. (For more information on the rule of thirds, see pages 34–35.)

SIMILAR SITUATIONS

Capture the seasons with these additional ideas:

Spring

- Stand *behind* a flower and snap your shot from that perspective.

- Buy a disposable waterproof camera and capture the fun of a rainstorm.

Summer

- Photograph a windsurfer on a nearby lake (if your camera has a "beach" setting, use it to help compensate for any possible overexposure).

- Capture a candid shot of loved ones in a hammock—use the trees to frame the picture.

Fall

- Take family photos with everyone dressed in colors that complement the leaves (green with red, blue with orange, and purple with yellow)

- Photograph leaves that have fallen to the ground—kneel down or crouch for a better perspective

Winter

- Capture the snow on the ground, but do it before anyone leaves footprints (if your camera has a "snow" setting, experiment with it)

- If you're taking pictures of an expanse of snow, shoot during early afternoon hours—in the evening, when the sun is low, you'll have more shadows that will gray the whiteness of the snow in the picture

[EMBRACE BAD WEATHER]

Author and artist John Ruskin once said, "Sunshine is delicious, rain is refreshing, wind braces us up, snow is exhilarating; there is really no such thing as bad weather, only different kinds of good weather." How true for photography! While it may seem like snow clouds and thunderstorms mean I can't go outside to take pictures, it's actually the opposite—I've taken some great shots by donning a poncho and braving the cold air.

 Annie's Approach:

- Instead of watching for sun to break through the clouds, head into the mountains so you're above low clouds on a rainy day. Wait for a patch of clouds to pass in front of you, then use it to frame a photo.
- Photographing clouds close to the camera makes the trees in the distance appear even farther away.

 Sande's Approach:

- When clouds are thick and the sun can only break through in small areas (called "sun spots"), the result can create an interesting dimension in your photos.
- Be patient—since you can't control Mother Nature, you may have to wait for several minutes (or even hours) to capture the perfect photo. Use a tripod to hold your camera so your arm doesn't become tired while you wait. Or, watch the movement of the clouds so you can estimate when they'll break and let the sun through.

Photograph by Annie Weis
Photograph by Sande Krieger
Photograph by Tracy White

 My Approach:

- You'll never find a rainbow without rain! Next time it rains, make sure you have film in your camera or an empty memory card. Once the rainbow appears, you'll need to photograph it quickly before it disappears.
- It can be difficult to capture the entire length of a rainbow without including homes or roads in the bottom of the picture. The solution? Find a nearby hill and head to the bottom of it, then shoot upward so you won't see the road.

Piha Beach

NORTH ISLAND, NEW ZEALAND

It was definitely worth the long drive from Auckland to catch the evening rays at Piha Beach.

PIHA BEACH **by Stacy McFadden**
> **Supplies** *Software:* Adobe Photoshop CS, Adobe Systems; *Patterned papers:* Scrapbook-Bytes.com; *Brads and overlay:* ShabbyPrincess.com; *Scroll brushes:* Stacy's own designs; *Computer font:* CK Magnificent, "The Heritage, Vintage & Retro Collection" CD, *Creating Keepsakes.*

Stacy's Approach:

- As sunlight breaks through the clouds, compose your picture so the sunlight points toward the middle of it. In this picture, the clouds seem to be moving to the right, and the roll of the hill downward to the middle of the picture helps draw attention to the beams of light.

- Experiment with light and dark contrasts. In this photo, the sun reflects on the water, making that section of the photo even lighter. The clouds produce an even darker setting over the already dark-colored grass.

SIMILAR SITUATIONS

You can also take interesting "bad weather" landscape shots when:

- It's raining. Be sure to photograph under a covered area where your camera won't get wet (such as from inside your car with the window down or under a pavilion that allows a wide viewing expanse).

- It's foggy or hazy. It adds a dramatic and mysterious look to your surroundings.

- It's windy. You'll be able to capture the movement of trees, fields and more. *Note:* If you're using a tripod, hang your purse or camera bag (or both) from the top to stabilize it and prevent the wind from blowing it over.

When my niece was young, she was fascinated by water; she loved looking at her reflection below her. You know what? She was on to something—that reflections create an eye-catching appearance. Reflections help me capture almost any landscape in a picture-painted look. They'll help you do it , too!

Photograph by Annie Weis

Annie's Approach:

- Place the edge of the water on a horizontal line one-third from the top or bottom of the photo. (For more information, on the rule of thirds, see pages 34–35).

- When deciding whether to place the water edge near the top or bottom of the photo, decide whether the water or sky looks better in a particular scene. Since the mountains appear small in this photo, including more water was the natural choice.

Annie's Approach:

- Don't forget about the reflections that appear at night, like reflections from the moon.

- When taking night shots of landscapes, turn off your flash. The range isn't far enough to illuminate distant objects, so using the flash will turn the background black.

- If you want to focus on the moon without any other landscape, wait to take your photo until the sun has been down for over an hour. If you'd prefer to focus on the scene as a whole, snap the picture within 40 minutes of the sun setting—the sky will appear as a majestic blue (instead of black) and the rest of the background scenery will still be visible.

Photograph by Annie Weis

Reflecting ....
...on crisp, dry air—so different from the heat and humidity of home;
...on the dramatic landscape—so unlike the flat farmland where we grew up;
...on the delicate leaves of the aspen—rewarding us with their last glow of gold;
...on treasured memories of our honeymoon—where do the years go;
...on clear mountain lakes—painting a beautiful scene in the mirrored surface;
...on massive mountains that surround us—a reminder of the grandeur of nature;
...on the rejuvenating peace we always find during time spent in the mountains.

REFLECTIONS **by Brenda Arnall**
> **Supplies** *Textured cardstock:* Bazzill Basics Paper; *Patterned papers:* BasicGrey (green dot) and Sandylion (burgundy crosshatch); *Circle punches:* EK Success; *Pens:* Pigment Liner, Staedtler; *Computer fonts:* Mostlios (title), downloaded from the Internet; Garamond (journaling), Adobe Systems.

Brenda's Approach:

- Up for a little exercise? Walk around the lake—the perfect shot may be waiting for you on the opposite bank.
- To frame the water with scenery (instead of using it to fill two-thirds of your picture), include nearby rocks or bushes in the foreground. Crouch down low and shoot upward if needed.

SIMILAR SITUATIONS

You'll find great reflections both in and out of nature. Look for these opportunities to capture them:

- Children jumping in puddles of water after a rainstorm
- Your husband fishing on a crystal-blue lake
- A couple sitting near a reflecting pond
- Teenage girls getting ready for prom by a mirror (you can capture both the front and back of their dresses and hair)
- Someone wearing sunglasses facing toward the sun (look at the scene captured in the lenses)

[SHOWCASE SUNSETS AND SUNRISES]

After a long day, there's nothing I enjoy more than sitting on my front porch and watching a glow-
ing sunset. Tranquility. Inspiration. Majesty. The warm colors bring all those feelings, feelings I
love to capture in my photos. I should know—I can hardly resist taking a sunset photo every time
the sky turns orange or red. To me, these skies capture everything in one word: beauty.

Photograph by Stacy McFadden

 Stacy's Approach:

- The sun will only be on the horizon for a moment—prepare before the sun sets so you're ready when it reaches the perfect height for your photo.

- If the horizon is speckled with trees, you can use the sunset to create a nice silhouette. Make sure the subjects you silhouette have easily recognizable shapes, so viewers immediately know what they are.

- By using a silhouette, you can re-create the feeling of a distant land from the comforts of your own home. Doesn't this photo make you feel like you're in an African savannah?

- Watch the sun throughout the day to follow its pattern—knowing where it should set will help you choose the best vantage point before the sun actually approaches the horizon.

 My Approach:

- A sunrise is beautiful near the ocean because of the way the light reflects on the water. If you're traveling near the beach, it's worth the effort to wake up early to capture beautiful photos.

- Use a tripod when taking your picture—since the light isn't bright in the sky, you'll need a longer shutter speed to capture the photo.

- A tripod will help stabilize the camera and prevent your pictures from looking blurry. Use the self-timer as well for extra stability so the camera won't shake when you depress the button.

- Arrive at your destination well before the sun rises—you'll want to be in position and have your tripod ready before the sun comes up. The earlier you are, the more chances you'll have for capturing all the amazing colors of the sunrise.

Photograph by Tracy White

My Private Sunrise

This was the view from the front porch in our new home when I woke up early one morning. It was certainly a reminder to stop and appreciate the beauty that surrounds us in everyday things and everyday moments.

MY PRIVATE SUNRISE **by Stacy McFadden**
> **Supplies** *Software:* Adobe Photoshop CS, Adobe Systems; *Patterned papers:* DesignerDigitals.com; *Brads:* ShabbyPrincess.com; *Overlay:* ScrapArtist.com; *Computer fonts:* CK Magnificent, "Heritage, Vintage & Retro Collection" CD, *Creating Keepsakes*; Typical Writer, downloaded from the Internet.

Stacy's Approach:

- To capture an array of colors in a sunrise, pull out your camera on a cloudy day. The more clouds you see, the more opportunities for the sun to reflect on them, painting brilliant colors across the sky.

- The sun doesn't have to be seen in your sunrise pictures. When clouds are in the sky, you'll see gorgeous colors as the sun approaches the horizon. (If it's too cloudy, though, you won't be able to see the sunrise at all.)

SIMILAR SITUATIONS

You can take a sunset photo wherever you go, but keep these tips in mind:

- Landscape shots—If you don't want the bottom of your landscape to appear as a silhouette, tip the camera downward when you meter the light, then aim it toward the sunset when you're ready to take the photo.

- City photos—See a beautiful sunset, but you're stuck in the middle of a city? Create a silhouette shot so passing cars or nearby phone lines don't detract from the brilliant colors of the sunset.

- Anywhere—Never look at the sun, even through your camera; it can still damage your eyes when seen through a lens.

chapter 5 holidays and special occasions

WHAT MAKES A SPECIAL OCCASION TRULY SPECIAL? For me it isn't just the "big" aspects, like the arrival of Santa Claus during a holiday parade or the grand city celebration on New Year's Eve. Rather, it's the little details that stand out in my mind: the wreath on my mom's door at Christmas, the cookies with red, white and blue sprinkles sold in stores for the Fourth of July, or a note left on my car for my birthday. Each of these small items helps me remember the meaningful moments of the occasion. And they're the props I use to take photographs that truly record my favorite memories of the day.

Whether you're celebrating a holiday, gathering for a reunion or celebrating the marriage of a close friend, you'll find numerous subjects at each event that will make for great photos. Look beyond, beneath and between the obvious to find something that captivated your senses or touched your heart. (Of course, don't get so caught up that you forget to capture the priceless, spontaneous moments or to make memories, too!) Your photographs—and scrapbooks—will be all the richer for it.

[SET THE SCENE WITH BACKGROUNDS]

While I absolutely love to journal in my scrapbook, occasionally I like to make pages with a title as my only text. In order to do that, I have to make sure my photo tells the rest of the story, revealing the location, the approximate date and the feeling of the moment. It takes a little more planning up front to make sure the background in my picture captures the setting, but it makes for some fun photographs, especially during the holidays!

 Candice's Approach:

- To add interest to your picture, include two seasonal items in the background. In this photo, the bale of hay peeking from the left side of the photo adds that extra charm that captures a more complete Halloween feeling than the pumpkins alone would have.

- If your seasonal items are low to the ground, you may need to take a shot from above your photo subject, looking down, so the items fill the background.

- Use a short depth of field, placing your subject between one and three feet away from the backdrop. It will allow you to capture the background without taking the focus off your photo subject.

Photograph by Candice Stringham

Candice's Approach:

- Include holiday decor in the background, but blur it slightly so the focus remains on your subject. Simply use the portrait mode on your camera.

- Black-and-white photos will also soften the effect of a portrait, especially when holiday lights are brightly colored.

- Use clothing to showcase your location. If you wanted to take this same shot with an outdoor feeling, putting a hat and coat on the boy would do the trick.

- For holiday events, make sure you have your camera ready the night before. When children are ready to open gifts, they won't want to wait while you load a new roll of film or head to the computer to clear your memory card.

Photograph by Candice Stringham

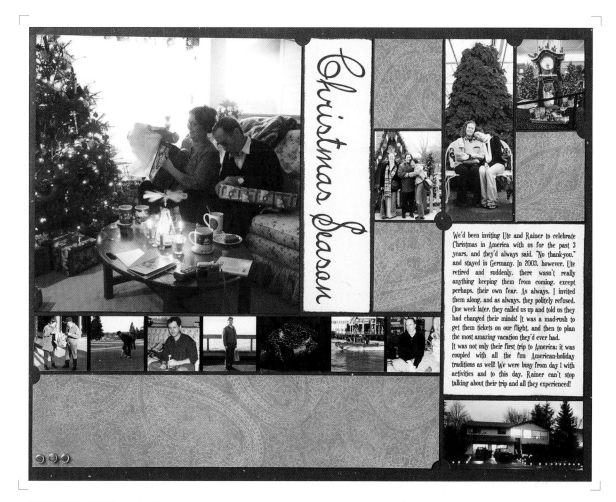

We'd been inviting Ute and Rainer to celebrate Christmas in America with us for the past 3 years, and they'd always said, "No thank-you," and stayed in Germany. In 2003, however, Ute retired and suddenly, there wasn't really anything keeping them from coming, except perhaps, their own fear. As always, I invited them along, and as always, they politely refused. One week later, they called us up and told us they had changed their minds! It was a mad-rush to get them tickets on our flight, and then to plan the most amazing vacation they'd ever had.

It was not only their first trip to America; it was coupled with all the fun American-holiday traditions as well! We were busy from day 1 with activities and to this day, Rainer can't stop talking about their trip and all they experienced!

CHRISTMAS SEASON **by Amber Ries**
> Supplies *Patterned paper:* PSX Design; *Computer fonts:* Euphorigenic and Bayern Handschrift, downloaded from the Internet; *Other:* Mini brads.

 Amber's Approach:

- A holiday setting doesn't always need to be placed in the background of your photo—you can also create a nice look by placing it in the same plane (at the same distance from the camera) as the people in the picture.

- When you tell a story in the background of every photo, you'll be able to capture the events of an entire season on a single layout.

SIMILAR SITUATIONS

Tell a story through your background with these additional items:

- Menorahs for Hanukkah
- Baskets of candy for Easter
- Flags or parade floats on Independence Day
- Gifts on a table for graduation, a wedding or a baby shower

[CAPTURE THE DETAILS]

The first holiday season I spent in my little home, I thought, "Oh, I live alone. I don't need to go all out for the holidays." So I simply set up my Christmas tree—sans lights and decorations.

But you know what? It didn't feel like the holiday season as much as it usually does. Why? The little details weren't there—the complete picture of my traditional holiday decor was missing. A few days before Christmas, I set up my remaining decorations, and it finally felt like the true holiday spirit was in my home. I always love those little details!

Farther away
Photograph by Melissa Chapman

 Melissa's Approach:

- If a macro shot (an extreme close-up) doesn't capture the setting, zoom out until it does. In this close-up shot, you wouldn't be able to guess what event the flower is from; in the zoomed-out picture, the shot still captures the flower's splendor while clearly showing that it was photographed on a man's tuxedo at a wedding.

- Let color contrasts add energy to your photo. While complementary colors are usually more pleasing to look at, contrasting colors catch viewers' eyes and pull them in. In this picture, the bright flowers pop against the black suit coat.

Closer-up
Photograph by Melissa Chapman

Melissa's Approach:

- Instead of photographing objects against a solid background, add interest to the picture by including part of a second backdrop, like the garden in this photo.

- Position long objects in a vertical line about one-third the distance from the edge of the photo. (Yes, we're revisiting the principle of the rule of thirds.)

 Sande's Approach:

- Use a short depth of field for close-up shots, but make sure you know the range your camera allows (you can find it in your camera's manual). If you're shooting an extreme close-up shot, consider using the macro mode on the camera.

- If you're shooting small objects that are transportable, move them near a window for the picture so you can use side lighting.

Photograph by Melissa Chapman

Photograph by Sande Krieger

SIMILAR SITUATIONS

Don't forget to capture these details, too:

- Buttons on the back of a prom dress
- Roses you received for your anniversary
- Horseshoes or gunnysacks used at a family reunion
- Bows on birthday presents

[ENHANCE FIREWORKS PHOTOS]

I love the Fourth of July—there's just something special about watching fireworks light the sky while listening to star-spangled music. It enhances my patriotism, and it reminds me how blessed I am to have the freedoms I do. I'm always awed by the city fireworks displays. In fact, since I want to capture every moment, sometimes it seems I watch them more through my viewfinder than not. The following tips will help you get great shots with fewer photos, so you can watch the rest of the display away from your camera!

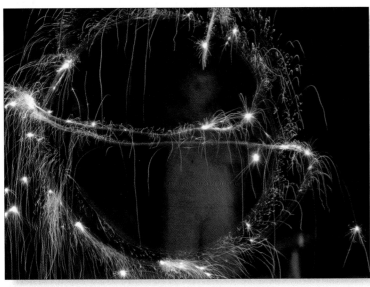

Photograph by Sande Krieger

 Sande's Approach:

- If you have manual capabilities, select a long shutter speed to capture the movement of sparklers. If you use a point-and-shoot, use the night mode and turn off the flash—the camera's shutter will stay open longer.

- Focus on the fireworks by using a depth of field that keeps them in focus while blurring the person in the background.

Photograph by Sande Krieger

 Sande's Approach:

- When you turn off your flash at night, your camera requires the shutter to remain open for a longer time (pictures are records of light, so they need to have light to record; at night, that requires a longer shutter speed). If your pictures ever turn out blurry, that's why. To get better photos, use a tripod to reduce camera shake while the shutter is open.

- Even when your camera is on a tripod, compressing the button to take your picture can make the camera move (again leading to blurry pictures). Utilize your camera's self-timer so you won't have to touch the camera when the picture is taken.

LIGHT IT UP! **by Melissa Chapman**
> **Supplies** *Textured cardstock:* Bazzill Basics Paper and Prism; *Patterned paper:* KI Memories; *Computer fonts:* PMN Caecilia 55 Roman and Sloop, downloaded from the Internet; Impact, Microsoft Word; *Other:* Brads.

The journaling on the layout reads:

Canada day was particularly important in Regina this year. We were also celebrating Saskatchewan's Centennial at the same time. Every year we have a fireworks display at Wascana Park that has proven to be quite disapointing. This year the city went all out. Fourty-one thousand people showed up for one of the best displays I've ever seen. Set to music, the firworks lit up the whole sky and lasted almost an hour. I was so glad I thought to bring my camera to capture a sight that will be hard to match.

 Melissa's Approach:

- Want to make every picture you take of fireworks look like it's part of the grand finale? If you can control your camera's shutter speed, leave it open for longer, allowing several different fireworks to be captured before it closes.

- As with any night shot, use a fast film speed (800 ISO or higher) when photographing fireworks for the best results.

SIMILAR SITUATIONS

These principles also apply when photographing the following:

- Light parades
- Children waving glow sticks in the air
- Candles at the table for a romantic Valentine's Day dinner

[WORK WITH LOWLIGHT SITUATIONS]

A few years ago, I held a surprise party at my house for a friend's birthday. Just after she arrived, the power went out because of a severe thunderstorm. Nice timing, huh? We didn't let it stop the party and continued by candlelight. At first some people thought it was unfortunate we wouldn't be able to take good photos since the lights weren't on. I disagreed. Instead, I let the lowlight setting with candles work to my advantage. As a result, I presented my friend with some memorable shots from her big day.

Without tripod
Photograph by Tracy White

 My Approach:

- Move the candle a few inches in front of your subject. The shadows on her face won't be as dramatic as they would be if the candle were directly below her.

- Turn off your flash—the background may appear darker, but your subject will look better.

- Don't have a tripod? Position your camera on a bag of beans (or another item that will mold around your camera and keep it steady when the picture is taken).

- Use a fast film speed, such as 800 ISO.

With tripod
Photograph by Tracy White

It begins with the ice, cold and sleek. A sheen glistens over the surface, almost matches the one in your eyes. There is a smell in the air, not quite January, yet colder than December. A big breath and then a step on the ice. It is shaky at first until the balance is reached. Then it is pushing and letting go. Gliding and turning and wind on your face. Freedom. Soon, everything and everyone becomes a blur. It is just you and the ice. This is the magic of *Skating* on the ice.

THE MAGIC OF ICE SKATING **by Gail Robinson, Photo by Julie Hess**
> **Supplies** *Ribbon:* Kirkland; *Photo corners:* Canson; *Thread:* Kreinik; *Vinyl ("Skating"):* Walls of Wisdom; *Computer fonts:* Palatino Linotype, Microsoft Word; CK Magnificent, "Heritage, Vintage & Retro Collection" CD, *Creating Keepsakes.*

Julie Hess' Approach:

- Compose your photo so the lit sections fill most of the frame. This will help your camera obtain more accurate light readings when it meters the picture.

- Meter your camera on something in the foreground, then aim it toward the lights in the distance to take your picture. This will help prevent the areas surrounding the object from looking black.

- Capture the movement of subjects in the foreground by turning off your camera's flash and using a longer shutter speed for manual cameras and the night mode for point-and-shoots.

- Use a tripod to reduce movement, which may otherwise contribute to blurry lights. Don't have a tripod? Lean against a solid object, such as a wall, fence or car. Take a breath right before taking your picture, then hold your breath while you snap the shot—it will help reduce your body's movement.

- Beware of standing under lampposts; their light can create a beamed look in the foreground of your photo or make it look overexposed.

SIMILAR SITUATIONS

You'll also want to compensate for lowlight situations when photographing these images:

- Candlelight vigils
- Luminaries lining a street
- Jack-o'-lanterns sitting on your front porch
- Party guests in a restaurant or pizza parlor
- Christmas lights shining on your home

[TAKE CHARACTER PORTRAITS]

Halloween is no dull time at **Creating Keepsakes.** *Every year, our entire team pulls out the all stops and comes up with the most clever costumes. Some of my favorites? A decathlon scrapbooker. A gothic Tinkerbell. And a coworker's dog dressed up as a skunk—unforgettable. With these great costumes, it's easy to capture unique and exciting pictures. My main objective is to make sure the shots are as creative as the people I work with!*

Photograph by Candice Stringham

 Candice's Approach:

- Little details are important for character portraits, so think ahead and gather everything you need, from costumes to props, before the photo shoot begins. This picture wouldn't be the same sans hat, glasses, purse and black gloves!

- To establish a sophisticated mood in your photos, use black-and-white film or its respective setting on a digital camera.

- You can create a sense of movement in your photo by using a longer shutter speed, such as that offered with the night mode on most cameras.

 Candice's Approach:

- Photograph your subject in a scene that matches the costume's theme. The extra few minutes of drive time will help you capture memorable photos.

- Does your character have any scenes that stand out in your memory? Re-create the moment for an added touch. Notice Cinderella's glass slipper a few stairs above her?

Photograph by Candice Stringham

GOOD WITCH, BAD WITCH by **Rhonda Stark**
> **Supplies** *Software:* Adobe Photoshop CS, Adobe Systems; *Patterned paper, chipboard letters and arrow:* Digital Design Essentials; *Computer font:* Script of Sheep, downloaded from *www.dafont.com.*

Rhonda's Approach:

- Have your costumed subject act the part of her role. If she doesn't normally show that personality, it will add humor to the photo.

- Close-up shots tend to appear "heavier" than shots taken farther away. When arranging your photos on a layout, place these pictures closer to the bottom of the page.

SIMILAR SITUATIONS

When photographing costumed subjects, consider these other photo ideas:

- Don't forget to photograph the back of the costume— it often shows fun details you won't want to forget

- If you can't get your little one to hold all the props, include them in the background of the photo

- If multiple photo subjects in a crowd dress up as the same character or as related subjects, make sure you get a group shot

- Halloween isn't the only dress-up time of the year— capture kids in costume during their play time or school plays, and photograph adults dressed up for theme parties

- Photograph your coworkers at an annual Halloween party

- Capture a child donning a Santa hat or a pet pup dressed up as Rudolph

[SET A SCRUMPTIOUS SCENE]

I can hardly resist a good piece of cheesecake at a wedding dinner or a warm roll at Thanksgiving. That's why photographing these delicious treats can be dangerous—the right photo will trigger my sweet tooth whenever I look at it! But I'm willing to make that sacrifice to capture the food; no layout about a special celebration would be complete without it. Besides, who said I can't eat a piece of cheesecake whenever I pull out my photos to scrapbook!

Photograph by Sande Krieger

Sande's Approach:

- When photographing close-up shots of plates and dishes, be sure to turn off the flash so it doesn't bounce off the glass and create an undesirable effect.

- Remember that not every photo needs to be of the finished dish—to tell the entire story of your celebration, photograph food preparations as well.

Photograph by Tracy White

My Approach:

- Think outside the box! Instead of photographing your famous homemade cookies on a plate, stack them for added interest.

- Crouch down to photograph food at eye level from the side. Since food is a commonplace item, you'll want to experiment with different perspectives and distances to capture it in an interesting way.

Candice's Approach:

- If the wedding cake is on a table with other decorations, make sure you balance them around the cake—it will add symmetry and stability to the photo.

- Turn off your flash when photographing wedding cakes. If your photograph is primarily white, the flash can make the background look dark, as it is here.

- Pay attention to the light above the cake. Fluorescent lights will add an unnatural green cast. When possible, open window coverings and use natural light.

Photograph by Candice Stringham

SIMILAR SITUATIONS

Remember the tips above when you're ready to photograph these items:

- Frosted Valentine's Day cookies

- Vegetable trays at get-togethers (Position red peppers along an intersecting point following the rule of thirds; since red draws more attention than other colors, you'll want to place it in the most dominant spot. For more information on the rule of thirds, see pages 34–35.)

- Dessert tables at a wedding reception

- Caramel apples lined up at Halloween

- Turkey on Thanksgiving (Keep in mind that meat doesn't always photograph well. Consider taking a picture of kids with the wishbone or carved pieces arranged on a platter instead.)

- A stack of latkes as part of a Hanukkah celebration

[TURN OFF THE FLASH]

Technology is not my forte. Whenever I start using a new gadget or software program, it seems like I make things harder than they need to be. Using a flash to take pictures of faraway objects is the same thing. Your flash only works for objects within so many feet (read your camera's manual to find out the distance for your specific model), so there's no need to use it for objects in the distance, like people on stage at a recital or concert. In fact, using the flash can often reduce the quality of these photos. So don't make your camera do any extra work—turn off the flash.

Photographs by Annie Weis

 Annie's Approach:

- Ask your subject ahead of time if the lights are brighter during one part of the concert versus another, then plan on capturing the best photographs during those times.

- Use your camera's zoom to capture your subject's facial expressions. To get the best shots, arrive early enough to get seats toward the front. If the front seats are below stage level, consider sitting about eight rows back so you're on a better level with the performers.

Without flash
Photograph by Tracy White

 My Approach:

- When photographing people close to you in a dark room, a flash will brighten their faces (often creating unflattering effects) and make the background appear pitch black. To avoid this, turn off your flash. Even if the photo is a little blurry, you'll be able to better capture the environment and setting.

- If you're sitting in an auditorium, use the arm rest to stabilize your arm when you take the picture. The more stability you have, the less likely you'll experience camera shake, which can result in blurry photos. (For more information on camera shake, see the glossary on page 102.) Take a breath before you take the picture or use the self-timer to help reduce the chance of camera shake as well.

SIMILAR SITUATIONS

Consider turning off your flash when snapping photos of these subjects:

- A band playing on stage at a concert
- Friends watching a movie together
- Family members sitting by a fire
- Luau happenings lit by tiki torches

With flash
Photograph by Tracy White

chapter 6 action

I'M THE FIRST PERSON TO ADMIT I DON'T KNOW MUCH ABOUT SPORTS.

I prefer scrapbooking or perusing handmade goods at a market over

watching soccer players throw touchdowns to home plate. Okay, so maybe

that's a slight exaggeration. But I do know one thing about sports—

photographing them is all about action. It's about the speed of the players,

the thrill of suspense before a game-determining play, the perfect swing

that drives a ball out of sight. It's about the moments that make the event

so memorable—and it's capturing these same moments that makes your

pictures memorable, too!

Photographing action takes practice, but you'll be able to enjoy many

unforgettable adventures along the way. Ready to get started? Call a time-

out from your daily routine and check out the tips on the following pages.

[GET CLOSE TO THE ACTION]

While traveling in Thailand, I heard the sound of drums start to fill the streets. Intrigued, I walked closer to the sound. The nearer I approached, the more I discovered about the music. I saw six players. I took a few more steps and realized they were young boys. As I got even closer, I discovered that their drums were not actual drums but makeshift instruments created from household items.

When I think back on the event, I'm grateful I walked closer to the action—it revealed more detail than I would have been able to notice from far away.

Photographs by Sande Krieger

 Sande's Approach:

- Get out of your seat and walk as close to the arena as you can. This way, the heads of the people in front of you won't fill your frame, and you'll be able to get a closer shot of the action.

- Place your camera on the gate or fence between the seats and the field—it will reduce the chance of camera shake, which is important for capturing action shots.

- Select a fast film speed (such as 800 ISO) and a high shutter speed to help stop or freeze the action on film.

Photograph by Sande Krieger

[PLAN AHEAD]

When the Olympics came to Salt Lake City, I had the chance to watch as the torch made its way toward the opening ceremony. I'd arrived early to make sure I had a good spot. I waited for the perfect moment when the torch approached, then snapped my photo—or I would have had I not forgotten to turn on the camera! My chance at capturing history had passed because I didn't check my camera beforehand. By the time I turned on my camera, the carrier had passed; I got a picture of the torch from behind, but not of the joy on the man's face as he ran. Lesson learned: Always plan ahead to capture the best shots.

 Sande's Approach:

- If your subject will be swinging a golf club, compose your frame ahead of time so you'll be able to fit it in the picture.
- Utilize the burst mode for action shots if your camera has one. It takes several shots in quick sequence, increasing your chances of getting the shot you want, such as the top of a golf swing instead of the beginning or end of one.
- Walk around your subject to find the best setting. Although you can't see the golfer's face in this shot, you can see colorful trees instead of the home and wire fence that border the golf course on the side behind the photographer.

Sande's Approach:

- If your subject will be following a specific course, find a nice location along the sideline and watch as he approaches. If you follow his pace, you can predict when he'll pass in front of your camera for the best shot.
- Use a tripod when you set up your shot so you don't accidentally move your camera when you look away from it to watch the swimmer approach.
- Can't stand next to your subject when he passes? Use a telephoto lens to capture a close-up shot.

Photographs by Sande Krieger

A LOVELY DAY **by Terrie McDaniel**
> **Supplies** *Patterned papers and cardstock flowers:* KI Memories; *Rub-ons and metal frame:* Making Memories; *Cards, photo turns and tape:* 7gypsies.

 Terrie's Approach:

- To capture faces, try to stand directly in front of your subjects. If your children are running along the beach, simply run a good distance ahead of them, then stop, turn toward them and set up your shot before they have time to reach you.

- In black and white, this photo appears slightly overexposed in the top-left corner because of the way the sun reflected off the water. To minimize this area and prevent it from detracting from your main subjects on a layout, cover the overexposed corner with accents or an additional photo.

SIMILAR SITUATIONS

You'll want to plan ahead when capturing these action shots:

- Divers jumping from the platform (Frame the shot with a vertical composition that lets you use the lines of the diving board and ladder.)

- Baseball players swinging a bat (Consider a horizontal composition if you plan to take the shot when the bat is facing the pitcher at the end of the swing.)

- Children performing their "big part" at a performance (Ask them ahead of time which section of the stage they'll be in, then find a location that lets you face that direction.)

- Runners approaching the finish line (Decide which is more important: getting a side view as they cross the line or seeing their faces by using a telephoto lens from the end of the track.)

[ZOOM TO CAPTURE EXPRESSION]

It's a good thing I don't play poker—I'm afraid I don't have a very good poker face. When I'm having a less-than-perfect day at work, my colleagues just need to take one look at me and they know it. Photos of me have the same effect as well. You can often tell what mood I was in when they were taken—if the photos are close enough to show my face, that is. If they're taken from far away, you wouldn't be able to read my expression at all. My advice? If you want to photograph someone's emotion, walk a few steps closer to your subject.

Without zoom
Photograph by Allison Orthner

Allison's Approach:

- When shot from far away, especially from the side, it's impossible to tell whether the subject is excited or frightened about her adventure.

- While this photo reveals the setting, the subject is small and gets lost amid the "white space" (here, it's green space) in the background.

Allison's Approach:

- Stand in front of your subject and zoom in to capture emotion.

- Let props set the scene. The helmet and ropes tell the story without needing to show the wooden pillars or zip line.

- If you have a long telephoto lens, stand as far away from the subject as you can while still maintaining a "close-up" shot. The farther back you are, the more your picture will look like you're on the same level as your subject when you zoom in.

- Be sure to get a photograph right after the action stops. Your subject will still show emotion, but the photo will be less likely to be blurry because the action is slower.

With zoom
Photograph by Allison Orthner

the
toddler's
creed:
when
all
else
fails...

{cry}

cameron,
age 1½.
trying
to
get
his
own
way.
toddler
style.

WHEN ALL ELSE FAILS . . . CRY **by Kah-Mei Smith**
> **Supplies** *Patterned papers:* American Crafts; *Stamps and rub-ons:* Fontwerks; *Stamping ink:* Brilliance, Tsukineko;
Pen: Zig Writer, EK Success.

Kah-Mei's Approach:

- Not all action happens on a sports field. Toddlers can create quite a show when they have a temper tantrum!

- Instead of positioning a subject's eyes on an intersecting point (using the rule of thirds), frame your photo to best capture the emotion. Here, the focus is on the child's pouty mouth. (For more information on the rule of thirds, see pages 34–35.)

SIMILAR SITUATIONS

You'll also find great facial expressions during these action events:

- A basketball point guard concentrating seconds before he shoots a free throw (*Note:* When photographing action indoors, use a high-speed film, such as 800 ISO or higher.)

- Football players after a touchdown is scored (whether by their team or the opposing team)

- Children running through sprinklers

- A baseball player sliding into home plate

- Kids jumping on a trampoline

- Friends bowling at a local alley

[TAKE MORE PICTURES THAN YOU NEED]

I used to be concerned about taking a large number of photos—after all, the cost of film and developing can add up quickly. Then I watched a photo journalist take pictures at a local event. Did he stop with one or two pictures? No—he used an entire roll in almost no time at all. When I picked up my prints, I had a few okay shots but none that I loved. I imagine the photo journalist had some so-so pictures as well, but with the number he took, I'm sure he ended up with some great photos, too.

I decided then that many of the events in my life may only happen once. It's worth it to me to use more film for additional shots if it means getting a picture I love.

 Candice's Approach:

- Capturing a picture of one person jumping in the air can be difficult—the timing has to be just right. Taking photos of multiple people jumping is even more difficult. The best solution? Take lots of pictures and you should end up with a few favorite shots.

- If multiple people are jumping into the air, balance them so the people who jump highest are in the center—it will allow the faces to create a visual triangle that's pleasing to the eye.

Photographs by Candice Stringham

BOO & SCOUT **by Tracy White**
> **Supplies** *Patterned paper and acrylic accent:* KI Memories; *Ribbon:* Making Memories; *Letter stickers:* American Crafts; *Stamping ink:* Clearsnap; *Pen:* Sakura.

My Approach:

- Want to know a secret? I took two rolls of film of my new kittens one day. Of those 48 shots, there are only 3 photos I absolutely love. It was worth the extra 45 photos to make sure I have these favorites, especially since my kittens will never be this small again!

- Experiment with different distances, locations and views to capture great shots. Be sure to bend down so you're on their level—even try lying on the ground!

- Animals are always on the go, so capturing them in clear pictures is no small feat. If your pet has a lull time during the day, take advantage of it to capture some shots while she's not moving.

- Side lighting helps you capture the best results. If you can control the environment where the action takes place, find a location that allows side lighting.

SIMILAR SITUATIONS

The more time an event lasts, the more pictures you'll be able to take. Consider these photo ops:
- Children playing at a local park
- Teenage boys practicing their skills at a skate park
- Soccer players using their heads to move the ball
- Golfers driving the ball to begin each hole
- Skiers practicing jumps for a competition

[MOVE WITH YOUR SUBJECT]

Believe it or not, I have a built-in special-effects tool for capturing images that say "action" with one glance. No, it's not part of my camera—it's my very own waist. Moving my upper body in sync with my subjects (a technique called "panning") allows me to capture them in focus while achieving a blurred background that creates a great action look. You can, too!

Photograph by Sande Krieger

Sande's Approach:

- If you want to capture action through panning, you'll need to choose your location before your subject approaches. Then select a lower shutter speed, such as 1/60—the night mode on most cameras works well. When he gets close, depress your shutter button and hold it while keeping your subject in the center of the camera frame until you release your shutter.

- Twist from your waist (instead of moving your whole body) to maintain stability and prevent camera shake.

- Turn off your camera's flash.

Sande's Approach:

- You can take great panning shots on amusement park rides. Since you're in the same vehicle as your subject, all you have to do is take the shot with a long shutter speed, like that used on the night mode. The subject will be moving in the same motion as you are, so he will be kept in focus.

- Try to time your shot so you start the pan when the background moves toward the sky (as the ride is rising)—it will make for a more aesthetic background than the pavement you'd see if the ride is on a downward slope.

- Remember to hold your hand still to keep your subject in focus. Consider using your camera's self-timer for added caution.

Photograph by Sande Krieger

Photograph by Angie Cramer

 Angie's Approach:

- For a unique perspective, photograph your subject with a pan from the front or back of the action, instead of from the side. You'll need to move with her in a smooth motion—consider riding in a car with someone so you can photograph her through your window (roll it down first). Make sure to wear your seatbelt and camera strap so you or the camera won't fall out.

- When it's safe to do so, have your subject look to the side so you can capture some of her face in the picture.

- You can create the same effect with an SLR camera by selecting a fast shutter speed and wide aperture—they blur the background while freezing the action.

SIMILAR SITUATIONS

Practice your panning technique by photographing these subjects:

- Joggers at the park
- Cars driving down the street
- Boats cruising on a lake
- A child moving down a slide
- Hockey players skating across the ice
- A dog chasing a stick

[SLOW THE SHUTTER SPEED]

One of my friends ran a marathon last year, so I couldn't pass up the opportunity to cheer her on. When the race started, the entrants took off at a good speed. I was impressed. As the race continued, these amazing runners kept up their pace! Their endurance was remarkable, and I wanted to get it on film. I could have taken the pictures on automatic mode, but that would have photographed only a brief moment of their motion. Instead, I used a slower shutter speed so I could capture the speed of the runners in action.

Photograph by Tracy White

 My Approach:

- Blurred photos show the motion of an event. Select a long shutter speed (which means the camera captures the picture for longer) so more of the action is revealed in your photo. The night setting is a good option to use.

- If you select a shutter speed slower than 1/60, be sure to use a tripod. Otherwise, your entire picture—not just the subjects' movements—may be blurry from camera shake.

 *My Approach:*

- You can heighten the feeling of motion by including a stationary object in the back-ground of the photo, like the balloon arch in this picture.

- Add drama and intensity to your action photos by kneeling down and getting close to the action when you take your shot.

Photograph by Tracy White

IN CONSTANT MOTION **by Sande Krieger**
> **Supplies** *Textured cardstock:* Provo Craft; *Patterned papers, acrylic accents and letters:* KI Memories; *Chipboard accent:* Scenic Route Paper Co.; *Flower:* Prima; *Stamps:* Postmodern Design; *Stamping ink:* ColorBox, Clearsnap; *Computer font:* Downcome, downloaded from *www.misprintedtype.com*; *Other:* Thread.

Sande's Approach:

- Not only does a long shutter speed reveal the movement of a player's swing, it also creates a sense of movement by showing the path of the ball. Use the landscape mode instead of the action mode, because the shutter speed will be longer.

- Add interest to your shot by composing it with the tennis net framing the bottom of the picture; it reinforces the setting.

- If you want to blur motion, consider using a slow film speed (100 or 50 ISO).

SIMILAR SITUATIONS

Consider using a long shutter speed when photographing these subjects:

- Wide receivers catching a football
- Baseball players up to bat
- Dogs jumping to retrieve a Frisbee
- Divers breaking the surface of the water on entry
- Gymnasts completing back handsprings
- Ice skaters spinning during a routine

[GLOSSARY]

Aperture: The hole in the camera lens (measured in "*f*-stops") that allows light to enter the camera and capture a photograph. With a wider hole (a smaller aperture), more light will enter, and vice versa. The aperture is a factor in determining depth of field. Larger openings give you less depth of field, while smaller openings give you more depth of field.

Camera Shake: Movement of the camera when the picture is taken that results in a blurry photograph. Camera shake can occur from even slight movement, such as depressing the shutter button. To avoid it, mount your camera on a tripod or place it on a sturdy object and use the camera's self-timer.

Depth of Field: The portion of the photo that is in focus. A large depth of field will have the entire picture equally focused; a smaller depth of field will capture the subject in clear focus and slightly blur everything in front of or behind it.

Exposure: The amount of light allowed on the camera's film/sensor and the length of time the light is allowed to fall on the film/sensor. Since the aperture controls how much light is allowed in while the shutter speed controls the amount of time that light is allowed in, an easy way to think about exposure is this: E = A + S (exposure equals aperture plus shutter speed). If you let in too much light—or overexpose—your picture will appear washed out, especially in the highlights. If you don't let in enough light—or underexpose—the picture will appear dark.

Fill Flash: Light source that fills in only the shadowed areas of a photo, as opposed to a regular flash that completely illuminates the main subject.

Film Speed: The speed or specific light-sensitivity of a camera, also known as ISO. Rated in numbers such as 100, 400, 800, etc. The higher the number, the more sensitive it is to light and the easier it is to capture movement. A higher ISO allows you to take photos in situations with lower light, though it generally means you will lose image quality. *Note:* Although digital cameras don't use film, their sensitivity is still calibrated using ISO numbers.

Flash Range: Optimal distance between your camera and subject to provide the right light in a photo. Check your camera's manual to determine the optimal distance for your specific model.

ISO: See Film Speed.

Metering: Used to calculate exposure by reading the light passing through a camera's lens. Most cameras have an in-camera meter—a reflected light meter—that measures the light reflected from a subject, then selects the aperture and shutter speed combination that will produce the best exposure for each picture.

Shutter Speed: The amount of time (measured in fractions) that light passes through the lens and into a camera. A small fraction (fast shutter speed) lets in a shorter amount of time than a bigger fraction (a slow shutter speed). A fast shutter speed will freeze movement while a slow shutter speed will cause a subject to appear blurry if he or she moved while the picture was taken.

Viewfinder: The eyepiece (or screen, for digital cameras) that displays the image the photograph will capture.

appendix

When you're taking photographs of your friends and family, you should take the special requirements of your subjects into account. For example, how you take a newborn shot will differ from how you set a shot of your fifth-grader. On the following few pages, you'll learn easy-to-use techniques for getting the best shots of your loved ones, no matter what their ages!

[BABIES]

Those precious first days of life are filled with moments you'll want to remember forever.
So make sure you get the best photos possible by keeping these basic tips in mind.

HELPFUL HINTS AT THE HOSPITAL

- Fluorescent lights typically give color images an unnatural green cast. And though it's more important to capture these first precious moments than it is to be preoccupied with professional photo quality, try shooting a roll of black-and-white film (with a high ISO) if you aim for more flattering hospital pictures.

- If you prefer color, take advantage of natural light if you have a window in your room. Turn the baby's face into the sunlight, then turn off overhead lights. The result will be a warmer photo without the green hue. And, again, film with a high ISO will help combat the poor lighting conditions.

HELPFUL HINTS AT HOME

- For photography that's easy on the eyes—and your baby—turn off the flash and use window light whenever possible. Not only is the bright light of the flash unflattering to babies, it's also unsettling to them.

- One of the biggest mistakes new photographers make is taking pictures too far away from the subject. Get closer! Cutting the distance will eliminate distracting elements and put the focus on the subject.

- Though it's natural instinct to photograph babies from above while they're lying on a bed or the floor, experiment with different angles. For example, lie next to your sleeping baby and shoot that cute little face from the side.

- Try holding the camera both vertically and horizontally before taking the picture. Choose the composition that eliminates the most distracting elements and best directs your attention to the subject.

POSING POINTERS

- Many formal portraits feature newborns propped up on pillows. While this is an effective technique, it can result in an unnatural look. If you want to prop, try the end of a couch or an armchair. Place a pillow just out of sight under the baby's tummy to help him feel secure.

- Just because Mom doesn't want to be in the picture doesn't mean she can't be near the baby! Have Mom lie on her back with her knees up. Cover her legs with a blanket that coordinates with the baby's outfit. Next, place the baby on Mom's legs. This pose allows the baby to "sit up," lets you get the camera in close and allows the baby to face Mom, one person he feels most comfortable with.

- If the baby is just a few months old—and can hold up his head, but not sit alone—try this pose: Have Mom sit sideways on an armless chair and hold the baby on her knee, supporting the baby with one hand on the tummy and one on the lower back. You'll be able to capture a cute, parent-free close-up of the baby.

- Try to capture a full range of your baby's expressions, not just the happy moments! Although those moods may be frustrating now, you'll smile later at your baby's grumpy, sad and petulant moods.

SMILE STARTERS

- Play peekaboo from behind the camera.

- Draw attention to a brightly colored toy that makes a soft noise.

- Attach an eye-catching black-and-white smiley face—with a cutout in the center—to your lens.

- Fan the baby with a small pillow or piece of cardboard. The sudden swish of air is typically greeted with a big grin.

- Rely on a stuffed animal, toy, expression or noise that always elicits a smile from your baby.

CLARA **by Alannah Jurgensmeyer**
> **Supplies** *Patterned paper:* Arctic Frog; *Rub-ons:* Making Memories; *Stamping ink:* Fresco, Stampa Rosa; *Other:*
Assorted ribbon.

[TODDLERS]

Getting your toddler to slow down long enough to take a photo can be difficult.
But, don't pass on capturing those moments—work with them!

HELPFUL HINTS

- Since your toddler is a whirlwind of activity, you must let go of the tripod and embrace a new approach. Consider how a photojournalist would attack an assignment: with a long (telephoto) lens so they can capture the action without being directly involved in it. (If you have a point-and-shoot camera, you can achieve the same effect by using your zoom.) They stay back, observe their subjects and try to grasp the essence of the situation with each shot they take. They don't direct, they capture … a great method for photographing toddlers.

- Toddlerhood is a time of exploration and a lot of firsts—even the mundane can be exciting when it's experienced for the first time. Be sure to keep your camera on hand at all times to catch these precious moments. Wait until your toddler is fully immersed in an activity before you snap a photo. These "everyday" shots can be even more precious than posed ones! Again, use the telephoto end of your zoom lens if you have one—you can get that great shot before your toddler even realizes you're taking a picture.

- And remember, for the best lighting, turn off your flash and use window light whenever possible. Add interest to shots by taking them from different angles, and don't forget to come in closer to eliminate distracting backgrounds.

- Work around your toddler's schedule. Even the greatest photographer is not going to be able to get a good picture of a toddler during a missed naptime. Choose an hour when he's most alert and happy.

POSING POINTERS

- Set everything up beforehand. Look at the light, figure out your exposure and—if you're setting up a backdrop or going outside—make sure everything is how you want it well ahead of time. Bring the toddler into your setup only after everything is ready.

- The most important trick to remember when taking a formal toddler picture? Keep him engaged. Use props and a setting that represents the toddler's personality. Props will allow him to focus on something other than the camera and hopefully keep him still for a moment.

- Give your toddler a general pose or a place to stand, then start shooting as she relaxes into it. As she gets more comfortable, she'll come up with cute poses and expressions on her own.

- To get a toddler to stand still, place a sticker on the floor and ask him to hide it with his feet.

SMILE STARTERS

- Puppets

- Animal sounds—make them yourself or name an animal and have the toddler give you the sound. This will keep him occupied and happy.

- Exaggerated sneezes

- Objects—such as Cheerios—hidden in props to keep toddlers focused on one spot

- Bubbles (but only toward the end of a shoot—after a short time, they'll insist on blowing the bubbles themselves)

Photograph by Candice Stringham

Photograph by Gaylene Steinbach

[CHILDREN]

Are you tired of the standard "school portrait" photos of your children? Try these easy techniques to capture their emotions and personalities.

HELPFUL HINTS

- Think about your fondest childhood memories. What did they involve and where did they take place? Do you wish you had photos of them? Sometimes capturing a moment on film for your children can begin by simply asking them about their favorite hobbies, events, occasions and friends. Take note. Then when you see those moments happening later, break out the camera.

- Just like seconds and hours make up our days, routines and schedules make up our lives. Don't forget to photograph the everyday moments in your child's day. They will be some of the most cherished memories years from now.

- To gather great ideas for photo-shoot locations, poses and lighting, look through children's clothing catalogs. Because they're released each season, they also reflect the hottest trends and color combinations of the day.

- Even the most beautiful child can look bad in harsh, outdoor light. Midday, for example, is not the time to have an outdoor photo shoot. Instead, opt for the early morning hours or try heading out a little before sunset. Both times of day give you nice side lighting. (Compare it to professional studio lighting—the photographer always has the lights a little above and angled from the sides.)

- When the midday sun just can't be avoided—at the zoo or a theme park, for example—it's time to use your flash. Yes, that's right! Many cameras have a fill-flash feature, which basically means it will fill in the dark spots and soften the harsh shadows the bright sun can create. Using it will help your subjects look their best on brightly lit, sunny days.

- Another technique to help on sunny days: simply look for some open shade. A partially enclosed exhibit at the zoo or a covered patio at an amusement park can be your answer to bad light and squinting eyes.

- Cloudy days are great for photographing people. The clouds serve as giant soft boxes for the sun that generate nice, soft overall lighting.

- Be patient. Give yourself plenty of time to get a good shot, and don't worry … even less-than-perfect pictures can successfully capture important memories!

Photograph by Sande Krieger

Photograph by Gaylene Steinbach

POSING POINTERS

- Asking a child to say "cheese" or smile for a camera rarely gets the natural result you'd like. Being unobtrusive will allow you to capture the spontaneous, candid moments that make up the joy of childhood.

- If you're trying to get a more formal photo, be sure to take a few candid shots before you ask everyone to pose. You'll discover that it's often these informal shots, rather than the posed ones, that become your favorites.

- Try a little give and take. Before setting up for a formal portrait, ask your child how he'd like to be photographed. Even if his answer isn't something you'd consider, give it a try. Not only might it result in a great picture, but after a few fun "his way" shots, you'll most likely get more cooperation when asking for the shots you want.

- Capture your kids in motion! Take several shots of them in action, one right after another. On some cameras it's as easy as holding down the button. On others, you can select the "burst" mode. The result may be an incredible sequence of shots.

- One mistake some photographers make in low-light, performance situations is to use the in-camera flash. Most flashes have a short range, making them ineffective from longer distances. Look in your camera's manual to determine the flash's range. It's typically about 14 to 15 feet—which means even if you're seated just a few rows back, your flash will light the back of the parents' heads in front of you and nothing on the stage.

- The best tip for photographing performances is simple: find out if your child's school is having a dress rehearsal and ask if it's okay to take pictures then. It'll give you a great opportunity to get some close-ups of your child without worrying about blocking other parents.

Photograph by Candice Stringham

Teens and adults are often camera shy. Make them more comfortable and help them look their best with these easy tips.

HELPFUL HINTS

- Most adults want direction, so offer guidance as you photograph them.

- It may help to have the subject tell you a story as you prepare the shot. For a happy picture, ask him to tell you about an embarrassing moment (which can illicit a laugh). If you want a serious portrait, ask him about something somber, such as what was on the news the night before.

- People have a tendency to keep tension in their shoulders when they're nervous or uncomfortable. To help your subject relax, ask her to shake her arms and shoulders a bit.

- If your subject seems to be particularly concerned about any "unphotogenic" features, study "Fixing Bad Features" below to give him more confidence about the results.

POSING POINTERS

- **Full Length.** A full-length portrait is terrific for showing an outfit and documenting a person's body characteristics. But unless the outfit is great or the background is truly exciting, the result can lack impact because of all the dead space on the sides.

- **Three Quarters.** The head, shoulders and torso view is common in the portraiture world. It's also not as intimidating to someone who shies away from the camera since you're farther away. The results, however, can often be lackluster.

- **Head Shot.** Taking a head-and-shoulders (or closer) shot is wonderful because you capture a sense of eye contact with the subject. It can be a little tricky, however, because you must capture the eyes in sharp focus and choose the correct lighting to be truly flattering.

LOOKING YOUR BEST

We all have that problem area—the one thing that causes us to dread having our picture taken. Never fear! Something as simple as a camera angle can help improve imperfections. The following tips will help you and your subjects feel better about being captured on film:

- **Long Nose.** If the subject has a long nose, have her face you rather than angling to the side. Use a softer light rather than direct overhead light that will cause a shadow from the nose and make it appear larger.

- **Stubby or Button Nose.** Have the subject drop her chin slightly. Never shoot from below.

- **Flyaway Hair.** Never backlight a subject with flyaway hair—it will give hair a "glowy" look, which will attract your eye to the frizz. Instead, move the subject so she's lit from the front. You can bring a dryer sheet (or hairspray and a tissue) to a shoot if you have a problem with flyaways—just run it lightly down your hair to tame loose ends.

- **Thin or No Hair.** Never shoot someone with a bald spot from above. Instead, shoot from slightly below and move away from bright overhead light, which will reflect or shine. Situate your subject in open shade, where the glare won't be as obvious.

- **Large or Heavy Body Type.** Avoid posing a person who is concerned about her weight standing straightforward toward the camera. Have her slightly angled at the shoulders toward the lens. For a slimming pose, have her place one foot slightly behind the other and place her weight on the back foot. Lines of contrast attract your eye, so also tell the subject to wear tone-on-tone clothing (pieces of the same color, but in slightly different shades) that will help draw attention away from the stomach area.

- **Short Body.** Shoot from below looking up with a wide-angle lens. Remember, with a wide-angle lens, whatever is closest gets stretched a bit, so posing legs closest to the lens can make them appear longer.

- **Tall Body.** If your subject is concerned about being too tall (in a group picture, for example), have her sit down and pose the others around her. If you are doing an individual pose, shoot from above to make her look smaller.

- **Double Chin.** A double chin can be hidden in many ways. One of the simplest methods is a "chicken or turkey stretch" or a "projection stretch." Have the subject point her face directly to the camera, then have her jut her chin forward. Though this may seem a little awkward, a photograph is two-dimensional and you won't be able to see the stretch in the photo. Another way to hide a double chin is to have your subject rest her chin on her hands. (*Note:* You only want the subject to lightly set her chin down so it isn't pushed forward.)

- **Ears.** Large ears or ears that stick out can be a big concern for some. The obvious solution would be to cover them up with hair. If the subject has short hair, however, turn her just enough so the ear isn't breaking the outline of her head—the angle won't draw attention to the ears.

SETH AND CHANDLER **by Shelley Laming**

> **Supplies** *Patterned papers:* Inviting Company (stripes), Manto Fev (ledger) and Anna Griffin (heart); *Number stamps:* PSX Design; *Letter stickers:* American Crafts and Doodlebug Design; *Stamping ink:* Fluid Chalk, Clearsnap; *Tags:* 7gypsies; *Photo corners:* Heidi Swapp for Advantus (pink) and Canson (tan); *Sticker:* Scrapworks; *Heart punch:* EK Success; *Fabric:* Amy Butler; *Die-cut quote:* My Mind's Eye; *Family definition card:* Jackie Bonette; *Other:* Mini brad and staples.

- **Glasses.** A simple way to solve glare is to push the frames slightly up at the earpiece. This tilts the lens slightly down and, while the difference won't be visible to the camera, it will dramatically cut the reflection.

- **Arms.** The easiest answer to the arm dilemma is to have your subject wear long sleeves, a much more flattering look.

- **Large Forehead.** Don't shoot someone with a large forehead from above, which will enhance the forehead and draw attention to it. Instead, shoot slightly from below.

- **Long Neck.** Shoot from a higher angle.

- **Eyes Not Matched in Size.** If your subject has one eye that appears larger on prints, remind her to open her eyes wide. You can also position the subject so the smaller eye is farther away from the camera, making it seem smaller because of the distance.

- **Hooded Eyes.** Hooded or deep-set eyes can look bad in bright sunlight because of harsh shadows. Use a reflector held right under the subject's face to bounce light up into the eyes.

- **Wrinkles and Age Lines.** Bright contrast light, like the sun overhead in midday, is the least flattering. In the middle of the day, the sun casts harsh shadows, which make wrinkles appear larger (not to mention increasing them from squinting). Try softer window lighting and a slight soft-focus filter. Having the subject look up and shooting from above may also help smooth wrinkles.

[GROUPS]

When working with groups, their positioning can be the most important part of the shoot.
Allow each subject to shine with these suggestions.

HELPFUL HINTS

- By putting people in a photograph together, you are implying some sort of relationship. Illustrate this connection through their arrangement. You wouldn't show two coworkers embracing, for example. Instead, they could be shaking hands. An engaged couple, on the other hand, should be embracing or leaning close together rather than standing apart.

- When coordinating a shoot for a couple or a family, ask them to coordinate the type of clothing they wear. You don't want some people in formal outfits while the others are in causal wear. Wearing similar colors will also help unify the group. At the very least, have them all wear dark, medium or light shades, which will have the same effect as wearing similar colors.

- Avoid shoulder-to-shoulder, "stiff," one-level posing. Instead, try creating levels or placing people in front of others. There are, however, two things to note when having subjects close together: take care not to have them too close (which will make them appear stuck together), and watch for hands (too many hands can look tangled, and all the flesh color in one place can divert the focus from their faces). Be sure to use space effectively to avoid these common traps.

- Overcome differences in height by seating taller subjects or shooting from above.

- When working with a lot of people, it's important to give them a focus. Have them look directly into the lens or at the top of your head so their eyes are looking in the same direction.

- With a really large group, try shooting from a high angle so everyone is looking up at the camera. This will allow you to see all the faces without having to pose people at different levels.

- If you have an extremely large group of people, consider dividing them for more effective portraits. For example, at a family reunion, pose each family individually rather than trying to capture them as one massive group.

- Keep the lighting as even as possible. Study each face to make sure the people in front are not casting shadows on the people behind.

- Shoot twice as many photos. With more people, there's more room for "mistakes," such as odd facial expressions, closed eyes, people looking in different directions or moving.

Photograph by Candice Stringham

Photograph by Candice Stringham

Photograph by Joy Uzarraga

[INDEX]